# EXPLRING the 50 STATES

## By Marcie Anderson

*for Lee*
*who gives me*
*encouragement*
*to start*

*and for my parents*
*who helped me*
*learn*
*to finish*

Cover illustration by Christy Russell Reed

Published by Willowisp Press
801 94th Avenue North, St. Petersburg, Florida 33702

Copyright © 1983, 1993 by Willowisp Press
a division of PAGES, Inc.

Printed in the United States of America

14  16  18  20  19  17  15

ISBN 0-87406-114-8

# CONTENTS

**ALABAMA (AL)**
**Capital:** Montgomery
**Flower:** Camellia
**Bird:** Yellowhammer
**Tree:** Southern Pine

**Nicknames:** Heart of Dixie, Yellowhammer State, Cotton State
**Admitted to Union:** December 14, 1819—22nd State
**Land Area:** 50,750 square miles (131,443 square kilometers)
**Total Area:** 51,609 square miles (133,667 square kilometers)
**1990 Population:** 4,040,587

# ALABAMA

Alabama is sometimes called the Cotton State. Once cotton was so important that it was called King Cotton. Today more soybeans are grown in Alabama than cotton.

Manufacturing is the most important industry. Important products include iron, steel, chemicals, paper, and plastics. Birmingham is called the Pittsburgh of the South for its heavy industry.

Montgomery was the first capital of the Confederacy during the Civil War. You can still tour the White House of the Confederacy where Jefferson Davis and his family lived.

Booker T. Washington founded a black college called Tuskegee Institute in 1881. George Washington Carver was a famous black scientist who taught there. He made more than 300 products from peanuts, including soap and ink. He made over 50 products from sweet potatoes.

Rosa Parks was a black woman who refused to ride in the back of a bus in 1955. This protest helped start the modern civil rights movement. Dr. Martin Luther King, Jr., was a civil rights leader who lived in Alabama for part of his life. He led a famous march from Selma to Montgomery in 1965.

Helen Keller was a blind and deaf girl who was born in Alabama in 1880. She learned to speak and use sign language. Later she went to college, wrote books, and traveled all over the world.

**INTERESTING FACTS:**
- The first American monument to an insect, the boll weevil, is in Enterprise.
- The Alabama Space and Rocket Center in Huntsville is the largest space museum in the world.
- The world's largest cave opening and the largest stalagmite can be found in Cathedral Caverns near Scottsboro.

# ALASKA

Alaska is the largest state in land area. It is more than twice as big as Texas. Its size is equal to one fifth of the continental U.S. Its coastline is longer than all the other states' coastlines put together. Alaska is the smallest state in population.

The native people of Alaska are the Aleuts, the Indians, and the Eskimos. Members of these groups still live in Alaska today.

The United States bought Alaska from Russia in 1867 for $7,200,000. That price was only about two cents an acre. Secretary of State William Seward arranged the purchase. Alaska was called Seward's Folly because most people thought it would never amount to much.

In 1896 gold was found in the Klondike region of the Yukon. In 1899 gold was discovered on the beaches at Nome. More than 30,000 people moved to Alaska during the Gold Rush to search for gold.

Alaska has many sights for tourists—mountains, volcanoes, sled dog races, totem poles, and glaciers. Mount McKinley is the highest mountain in the U.S. There are more kinds of big game in Alaska than in any other state. Alaska has black bears, grizzly bears, polar bears, moose, caribou, elk, mountain goats, and wolves. There are also many fur-bearing animals.

The main industries in Alaska are oil and gas. The

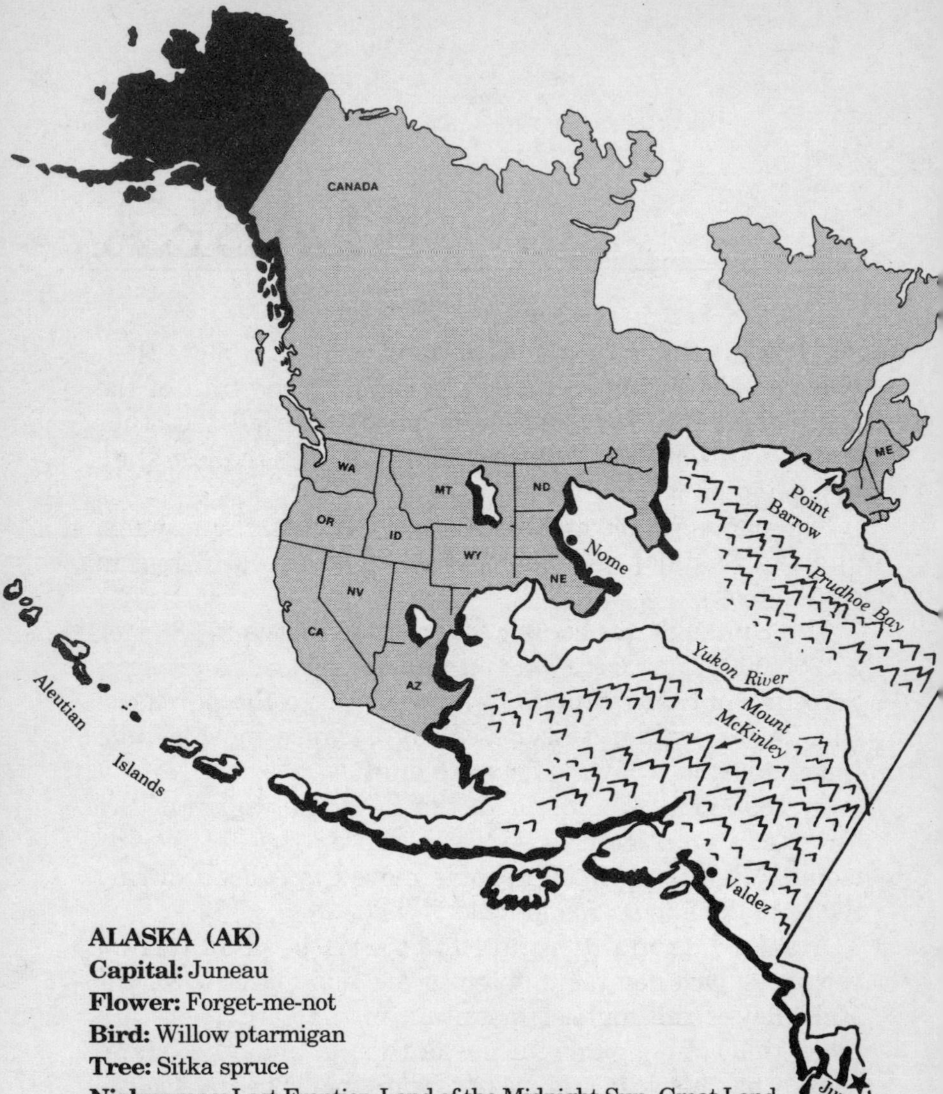

CANADA

WA

OR

ID

MT

ND

WY

NE

NV

CA

AZ

Nome

Point
Barrow

Prudhoe Bay

ME

Yukon River

Mount
McKinley

Valdez

Aleutian

Islands

Juneau

**ALASKA (AK)**
**Capital:** Juneau
**Flower:** Forget-me-not
**Bird:** Willow ptarmigan
**Tree:** Sitka spruce
**Nicknames:** Last Frontier, Land of the Midnight Sun, Great Land
**Admitted to Union:** January 3, 1959—49th State
**Land Area:** 570,374 square miles (1,467,059 square kilometers)
**Total Area:** 589,757 square miles (1,527,464 square kilometers)
**1990 Population:** 550,043

8

Prudhoe Bay reservoir of oil and gas is twice as large as any other reservoir in North America. The Trans-Alaska pipeline carries oil 800 miles from Prudhoe Bay to the port of Valdez. Other important industries are fisheries, wood, and furs.

Alaska is sometimes called the Land of the Midnight Sun. The summer sun shines for about 20 hours a day in the central part of the state. In the winter Fairbanks has only four hours of sun.

## INTERESTING FACTS:

- The strongest earthquake in North America hit Alaska in 1964. It caused 117 deaths and damage of $600 million. The earthquake was followed by a seismic wave 50 feet high that traveled 8,445 miles at 450 miles per hour.
- The Aleutian Islands are the western most point in the U.S. The northern most point is Point Barrow.
- Alaska's state flag was designed in 1926 by Benny Benson, a 13-year-old orphan. It shows the Big Dipper and the North Star on a blue background.

**ARIZONA (AZ)**
**Capital:** Phoenix
**Flower:** Saguaro cactus blossom
**Bird:** Cactus wren
**Tree:** Paloverde
**Nickname:** Grand Canyon State
**Admitted to Union:** February 14, 1912—48th State
**Land Area:** 113,417 square miles (293,750 square kilometers)
**Total Area:** 114,000 square miles (296,400 square kilometers)
**1990 Population:** 2,717,866

# ARIZONA

Arizona is famous for its pleasant weather. The days are warm, dry, and sunny. The nights are cool. The air is "so clear that cowboys can see a girl wink a mile away."

Spanish explorers came to Arizona in the 1500s looking for gold. Missionaries followed and started settlements. Arizona was owned by Spain and Mexico until it was purchased by the U.S. in 1853.

Arizona was an important part of the Old West. Many Indian tribes lived there. Today more Indians live in Arizona than in any other state except Oklahoma and California. Members of 13 tribes live on 20 Indian reservations.

The Grand Canyon is the largest canyon in the world. It is 277 miles (349 kilometers) long, 600 feet to 18 miles (6.4 to 22.5 kilometers) wide, and one mile (1.6 kilometers) deep. The Colorado River flows through the canyon.

Manufacturing and agriculture are Arizona's most important industries. Over half the nation's copper is produced in this state. Cotton is the most important crop. Arizona also produces lettuce and other salad ingredients. Sometimes Arizona is called the Salad Bowl of the Nation.

Phoenix, the capital, is named for a mythical bird that rose from the ashes of a fire to live again.

The world's biggest dam is the New Cornelia Tailings near Ajo. The Hoover Dam is another large dam in Arizona.

Water is scarce in Arizona and has to be conserved.

This state has many unusual plants and animals. Many kinds of cacti live in the desert. There are mountain lions, bobcats, wild horses and burros, and coyotes. The Gila monster is the only poisonous lizard in the U.S.

## INTERESTING FACTS:

- London Bridge was moved to Lake Havasu in 1967. The granite bridge weighs ten thousand tons.
- The Gunfight at the OK Corral took place in 1881. The Earp brothers and Doc Holiday fought the Clantons.
- The world's largest rosebush has been growing in Tombstone since 1884. Its trunk is more than 40 inches (101.6 centimeters) thick.
- An old legend says that anyone who drinks from the Hassayampa River will never tell the truth again.

# ARKANSAS

Hernando de Soto first explored Arkansas in 1541. Father Marquette, Joliet, and La Salle were other explorers of this state. Arkansas became part of the U.S. with the Louisiana Purchase.

During the early 1800s cotton was planted in Arkansas. The climate and soil were perfect for huge cotton plantations. The cotton was picked by slaves. Arkansas was part of the Confederacy in the Civil War. The battles of Pea Ridge and Prairie Grove were fought in Arkansas.

Cotton is still the major crop in Arkansas. The state is also a leading producer of rice and soybeans. Arkansas produces 97 percent of the nation's bauxite ore. It is used to make aluminum.

Hot Springs National Park is a popular tourist spot. The waters there have an average temperature of 143°F (62°C). You can bathe in the warm spring waters at Bathhouse Row. Some people think the minerals in the water are helpful for aches and pains.

The only diamond field in the U.S. is in Crater of Diamonds State Park near Murfreesboro. You can hunt for diamonds there. About two diamonds a day are found. The biggest diamond found was worth a quarter of a million dollars. It's called the Uncle Sam diamond.

The Ozark Mountains are a region known for folk arts and crafts. Ozark mountain people make cornhusk dolls,

**ARKANSAS (AR)**
**Capital:** Little Rock
**Flower:** Apple blossom
**Bird:** Mockingbird
**Tree:** Pine
**Nickname:** Land of Opportunity
**Admitted to Union:** June 15, 1836—25th State
**Land Area:** 52,075 square miles (134,875 square kilometers)
**Total Area:** 53,104 square miles (137,539 square kilometers)
**1990 Population:** 2,350,725

fiddles, baskets, and quilts. They remember the songs and dances of their ancestors. They learned their skills from their parents and grandparents.

Blanchard Springs Caverns are huge caves with unusual rock formations. An elevator takes you down to the caves.

## INTERESTING FACTS:

- The oldest newspaper west of the Mississippi is the *Arkansas Gazette*. It was founded in 1819.
- Some of the drinking fountains in the city of Hot Springs are unusual. The water comes out hot!
- Arkansas is the only state with a law on the correct way to say its name. It is ARK-an-saw.

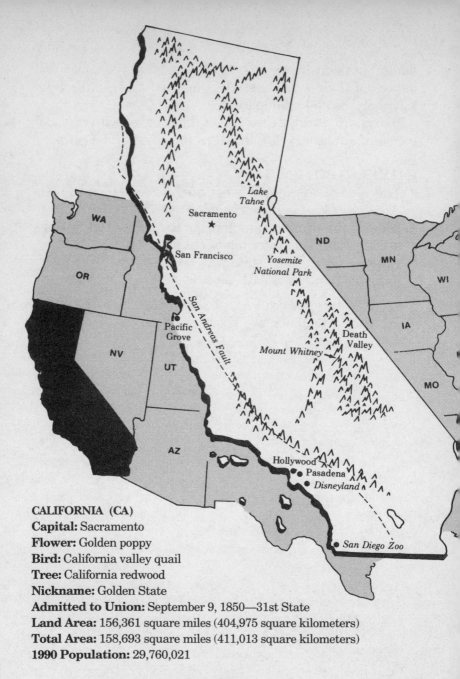

**CALIFORNIA (CA)**
**Capital:** Sacramento
**Flower:** Golden poppy
**Bird:** California valley quail
**Tree:** California redwood
**Nickname:** Golden State
**Admitted to Union:** September 9, 1850—31st State
**Land Area:** 156,361 square miles (404,975 square kilometers)
**Total Area:** 158,693 square miles (411,013 square kilometers)
**1990 Population:** 29,760,021

16

# CALIFORNIA

There are more people in California than in any other state. The number of people in the state doubled every 20 years for over a century. Los Angeles is the second largest city in the U.S.

Thousands of people moved to California after gold was discovered in 1848. The biggest gold strike in U.S. history was near Sutter's Mill.

President Lincoln made Yosemite Valley the first state park in 1864. Almost one fourth of California's land belongs to state or national parks or forests. The world's tallest trees, redwoods and sequoias, are found in California. The largest living sequoia is the General Sherman Tree. It is 3,500 years old.

The lowest point in the U.S. is at Death Valley, which is 282 feet (about 86 meters) below sea level. Mount Whitney is the state's highest mountain. Beautiful Lake Tahoe is one of the deepest lakes in the U.S. There are about eight thousand lakes in California.

The San Andreas Fault is a weak place in the earth that runs along the coast of California. This makes earthquakes likely in the state. In 1906 an earthquake and fires caused terrible damage to San Francisco. Five hundred people were killed. The business section of the city was destroyed. On October 17, 1989, the San Francisco area experienced another major earthquake. This quake measured 7.1 on the richter scale and caused billions of dollars of damage. Over 100,000 buildings were damaged or destroyed. Sixty-seven people were killed and over 3,000 were injured.

Tourism is a big industry in this state. Disneyland, San Francisco, and Hollywood are all popular for vacations. Other famous things to see are Yosemite Falls at Yosemite National Park, the San Diego Zoo, and the Rose Bowl football game and parade held every January in Pasadena.

California leads the nation in electronics, aerospace, and agriculture. Almost half the country's fruits and nuts are grown here. One quarter of all the vegetables sold in the U.S. are grown in California.

**INTERESTING FACTS:**
- The state fossil is the saber-toothed cat. The state insect is the California dog-faced butterfly, also called the flying pansy.
- In Pacific Grove it is illegal to kill or even annoy or disturb a butterfly. The town is a nesting grove for monarch butterflies.
- Mark Twain wrote a story called "The Celebrated Jumping Frog of Calaveras County." A frog jumping contest is still held every year in Calaveras County.

# COLORADO

There are 17 mountain groups and ranges in Colorado. The Rocky Mountains include more than 1,000 mountains over 10,000 feet (3,048 meters) high. Pikes Peak is the most famous Colorado mountain. Zebulon Pike discovered it in 1806.

The Rocky Mountains are popular with skiers. Aspen, Vail, and Steamboat Springs are resort skiing towns. Tourists enjoy visiting the U.S. Air Force Academy near Colorado Springs.

At Mesa Verde National Park you can tour Pueblo Indian houses built in the sides of cliffs. They were built over 1,000 years ago. One ruin called Cliff Palace has 200 rooms built on eight levels.

You can see dinosaur fossils at Dinosaur National Park. Many kinds of dinosaurs lived in Colorado.

Denver is called the Mile-High City because it is over 5,000 feet (1,524 meters) above sea level. Colorado's capitol building in Denver is patterned after the U.S. Capitol. Its dome is covered with a thin layer of gold.

There were several gold rushes in Colorado after 1859. Many settlers had signs on their wagons saying, "Pikes Peak or bust." The Cripple Creek region of gold mines has produced over $400 million in gold. There were also many silver mines in frontier days.

Mining is still a major industry in Colorado. Gold, silver,

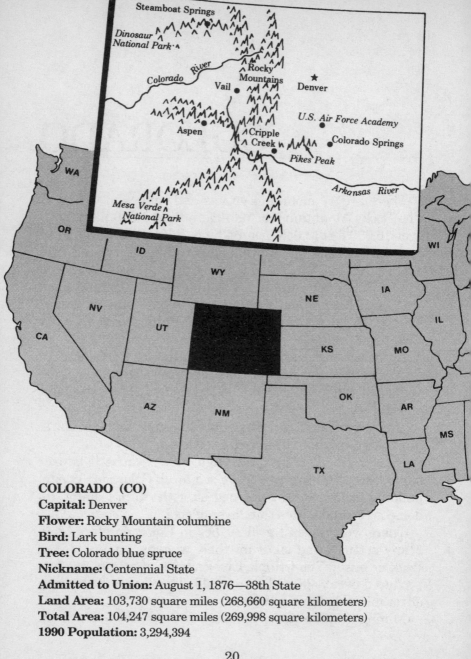

**COLORADO (CO)**
**Capital:** Denver
**Flower:** Rocky Mountain columbine
**Bird:** Lark bunting
**Tree:** Colorado blue spruce
**Nickname:** Centennial State
**Admitted to Union:** August 1, 1876—38th State
**Land Area:** 103,730 square miles (268,660 square kilometers)
**Total Area:** 104,247 square miles (269,998 square kilometers)
**1990 Population:** 3,294,394

tin, lead, zinc, and uranium are mined today. Manufacturing is now the state's most important industry. Other industries are agriculture, cattle, sheep, and tourism. Millions of tourists visit the state each year.

Colorado is called the Centennial State. It became a state in 1876. The U.S. celebrated its centennial, or hundredth birthday, that year.

## INTERESTING FACTS:

- Some of Colorado's mountain ranges have unusual names: the Mummy Range, the Never Summer Range, the Mosquito Range, the Rabbit Ear Range, and the Wet Mountains.
- Katherine Lee Bates wrote the song "America the Beautiful" after a trip to the top of Pikes Peak.
- Two of Colorado's famous frontier scouts were Kit Carson and Buffalo Bill Cody.

**CONNECTICUT (CT)**
**Capital:** Hartford
**Flower:** Mountain laurel
**Bird:** Robin
**Tree:** White oak
**Nicknames:** Constitution State, Nutmeg State
**Admitted to Union:** January 9, 1788—5th State
**Land Area:** 4,862 square miles (12,593 square kilometers)
**Total Area:** 5,009 square miles (12,973 square kilometers)
**1990 Population:** 3,287,116

# CONNECTICUT

A Connecticut Yankee is a smart person who can get hard things done. People from this state are famous for their inventions and businesses. In colonial days, Connecticut manufactured most of its own products, such as nails, axes, and combs. This state had some of the first U.S. factories, including the first ax, hat, and bicycle factories. Other Connecticut businesses were famous for clocks, firearms, ammunition, ship building, engines, and bells. Some famous business pioneers were Eli Whitney, Samuel Colt, and Charles Goodyear.

Connecticut has over 1,000 houses built before the American Revolution. Many are open for tours. Several famous men of the Revolutionary War were from this state: General Israel Putnam, Roger Sherman, and Ethan Allen. Nathan Hale was a teacher from New London who was executed by the British for spying. His last words were "I regret that I have but one life to give for my country."

This state was an important shipping center in the 1700s and 1800s. The Mystic Seaport Museum recreates a New England coastal village of the 1800s. You can see an old whaling ship there. Some ships are still built in the state. The world's first nuclear-powered submarine, the *Nautilus,* was built at Groton in 1954.

Hartford is known as the Insurance City because many insurance companies are located there. The oldest daily newspaper in the U.S. with the same name is the *Hartford Courant*. It was started in 1764.

Today Connecticut is a leader in the manufacturing of metal products. Tourism and agriculture are also important. In Connecticut a special kind of tobacco is grown under the shade of cloth tents. It is the most valuable crop per acre in the U.S. It is used to wrap cigars.

## INTERESTING FACTS:
- Mark Twain lived in Hartford for 17 years. He wrote Tom Sawyer and Huckleberry Finn while living there.
- "Yankee Doodle Dandy" is the state song. It was written about some Connecticut men serving in the French and Indian War.
- The Lock Museum of America is in Terryville. It owns over 10,000 locks and keys made in Connecticut over 100 years ago.

# DELAWARE

Thomas Jefferson gave Delaware its nickname of the Diamond State because of all its riches. Delaware is called the First State because it was the first state to ratify (accept) the constitution.

Delaware is the second smallest state. But more large companies have their headquarters in Delaware than in any other state. Delaware laws are very favorable to business.

The du Pont family has held an important place in Delaware's history. The du Pont brothers started a gunpowder mill near Wilmington in 1802. The company continued to grow and to produce many kinds of chemicals. Delaware is sometimes called the Chemical Capital of the World because of this.

Today the Du Pont Corporation is one of the nation's largest. Its chemical factories and research centers are some of the largest in the world. The company makes many chemicals and synthetic materials like Orlon, Dacron, and Teflon. In 1977, Pierre S. du Pont IV was elected the governor of the state.

Delaware was a pioneer in the food-canning industry. Jell-O is produced in Dover. The state's farms produce chickens, corn, soybeans, and other crops. Manufacturing and fishing are other major industries.

The Chesapeake and Delaware Canal cuts across the northern tip of the state. It connects Delaware Bay and Chesapeake Bay.

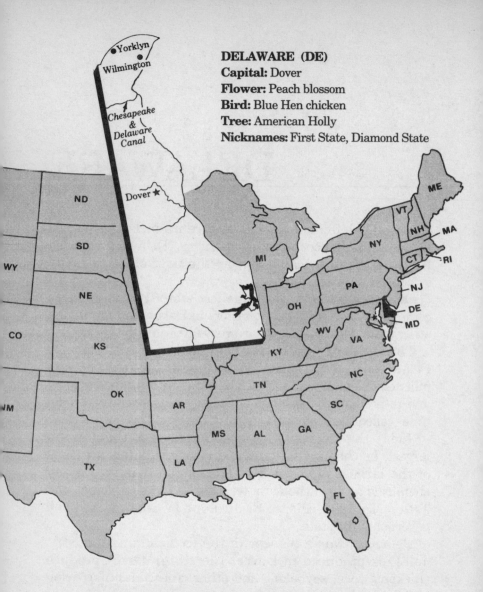

**DELAWARE (DE)**
**Capital:** Dover
**Flower:** Peach blossom
**Bird:** Blue Hen chicken
**Tree:** American Holly
**Nicknames:** First State, Diamond State

**Admitted to Union:** December 7, 1787—1st State
**Land Area:** 1,982 square miles (5,133 square kilometers)
**Total Area:** 2,057 square miles (5,328 square kilometers)
**1990 Population:** 666,168

**INTERESTING FACTS:**
- The state insect is the ladybug.
- The oldest business in the U.S. is the J. E. Rhoads Corporation in Wilmington. It began making leather goods in 1702.
- The Steam Museum in Yorklyn has a miniature railroad with steam engines and locomotives. It also has a large collection of steam-powered automobiles.

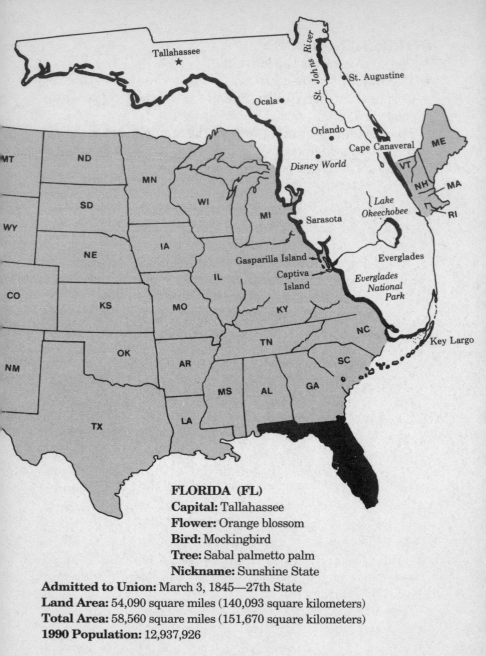

**FLORIDA (FL)**
**Capital:** Tallahassee
**Flower:** Orange blossom
**Bird:** Mockingbird
**Tree:** Sabal palmetto palm
**Nickname:** Sunshine State
**Admitted to Union:** March 3, 1845—27th State
**Land Area:** 54,090 square miles (140,093 square kilometers)
**Total Area:** 58,560 square miles (151,670 square kilometers)
**1990 Population:** 12,937,926

# FLORIDA

Ponce de Leon claimed Florida for Spain in 1513. He was searching for the mythical Fountain of Youth. Spain sold Florida to the U.S. in 1819.

The oldest permanent city in the U.S. is St. Augustine. It was founded in 1565. The oldest masonry fort in the U.S. is a castle there called Castillo de San Marcos.

Florida's sunny weather and beautiful beaches attract millions of tourists a year. You can visit a circus museum in Sarasota. You can get splashed by a killer whale at Sea World near Orlando. You can learn about space exploration at the Kennedy Space Center in Cape Canaveral. And don't forget the world's largest tourist attraction—Disney World near Orlando.

The Everglades, one of the largest swamp areas in the world, is located in the southern part of Florida. Part of the Everglades was made into a National Park area. Everglades National Park is a large nature preserve. Alligators, crocodiles, turtles, manatees, snakes, lizards, and insects live there.

Florida is a large peninsula. On its east coast is the Atlantic Ocean. On its west coast is the Gulf of Mexico. More kinds of fish live in Florida waters than anywhere else in the world.

Florida's leading industries are agriculture, tourism, and manufacturing. Citrus fruits, sugarcane, vegetables, and other crops like corn are big business in Florida. Fishing, forestry, and cattle raising are also important.

There are many tales told about pirates, shipwrecks, and buried treasure in Florida. Gasparilla Island was named for the pirate José Gaspar. Captiva Island got its name from all the pirates held captive there.

## INTERESTING FACTS:
- You can watch the fish through a glass-bottomed boat at Silver Springs near Ocala. The springs produce five hundred million gallons (nearly two billion liters) of water a day.
- The Museum of Yesterday's Toys in St. Augustine has toys dating back to the 1600s. There are over 4,500 dolls on display.
- The only underwater state park in the U.S. is off Key Largo. If you're a scuba diver, you can visit the John Pennekamp Coral Reef State Park.
- In August 1992, Hurricane Andrew struck the Bahamas, south Florida, and Louisiana. The damage in Florida alone was estimated at $20.6 billion, making Andrew the most costly U.S. hurricane up to that point.

# GEORGIA

Georgia is the largest state in land area east of the Mississippi River. It is famous for its peanuts and peaches. Plains, Georgia, is the home of the thirty-ninth U.S. president, Jimmy Carter.

Eli Whitney invented the cotton gin in Georgia in 1793.This machine separated the seeds from cotton. It helped make the crop "King Cotton" in the South.

The US. government forced the Cherokee Indians to leave Georgia between 1835 and 1838. More than 13,000 Cherokees were marched to reservations in Oklahoma. Many of them died along the way. Their route is still called the Trail of Tears.

Georgia fought for the South in the Civil War. Several battles were fought in the state. General Sherman invaded Georgia and burned Atlanta. His march through Georgia ended in Savannah in 1864.

Atlanta is Georgia's capital and largest city. Its airport is the second busiest in the world. Atlanta is the communications and transportation center for the southeast U.S. The black civil rights leader, Dr. Martin Luther King, Jr., is buried there.

Georgia leads the nation in producing paper, boards, and turpentine. Important crops are corn, cotton, and tobacco.

Stone Mountain Park, east of Atlanta, has a game ranch and restored plantation. Stone Mountain is one of the

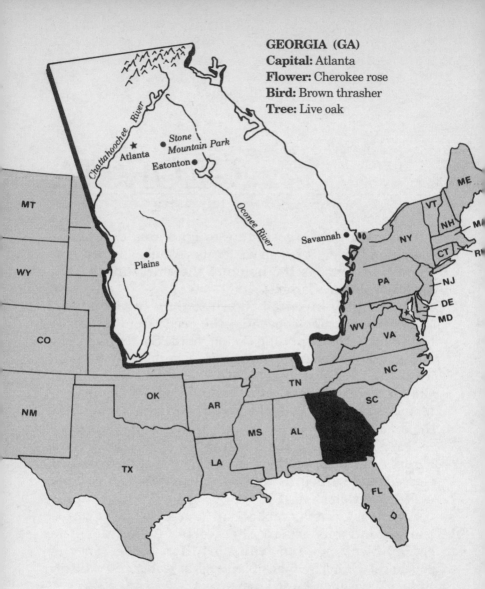

**GEORGIA (GA)**
**Capital:** Atlanta
**Flower:** Cherokee rose
**Bird:** Brown thrasher
**Tree:** Live oak

**Nicknames:** Peach State, Empire State of the South
**Admitted to Union:** January 2, 1788—4th State
**Land Area:** 58,073 square miles (150,409 square kilometers)
**Total Area:** 58,876 square miles (152,488 square kilometers)
**1990 Population:** 6,478,216

32

largest exposed granite masses in North America. It has the world's largest sculpture. The profiles of Robert E. Lee, Stonewall Jackson, and Jefferson Davis on their horses are carved into granite on the side of the mountain. You can ride a cable car to the top of the mountain.

## INTERESTING FACTS:
- A huge statue of Br'er Rabbit stands on the courthouse lawn in Eatonton. Joel Chandler Harris made Br'er Rabbit famous in his Uncle Remus tales.
- You can visit the Jimmy Carter Library and Museum in Atlanta.
- You can tour Juliette Gordon Low's home in Savannah. She founded the Girl Scouts of the U.S.A.
- The first surgical operation using ether was performed in Georgia in 1842. Dr. Crawford W. Long was the surgeon.

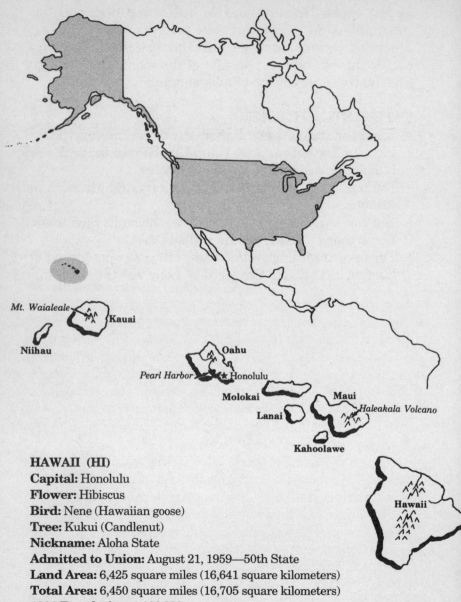

Mt. Waialeale

Kauai

Niihau

Oahu

Pearl Harbor ★ Honolulu

Molokai

Maui

Lanai

Haleakala Volcano

Kahoolawe

**HAWAII (HI)**
**Capital:** Honolulu
**Flower:** Hibiscus
**Bird:** Nene (Hawaiian goose)
**Tree:** Kukui (Candlenut)
**Nickname:** Aloha State
**Admitted to Union:** August 21, 1959—50th State
**Land Area:** 6,425 square miles (16,641 square kilometers)
**Total Area:** 6,450 square miles (16,705 square kilometers)
**1990 Population:** 1,108,229

Hawaii

# HAWAII

Hawaii was first settled in the sixth century. Polynesians sailed from other Pacific islands to settle there. Captain James Cook visited Hawaii in 1778. He called the Hawaiian Islands the Sandwich Islands.

King Kamehameha I united the islands in 1795. King Kalakaua finished building the Iolani Palace in Honolulu in 1880. After he died, his sister became Queen Liliuokalani. She lived in the palace and ruled for two years. In 1894 Hawaii became a republic and the palace was its capitol. Hawaii became a U.S. territory in 1900.

Hawaii is made up of over 100 islands. People live on the eight largest islands: Hawaii, Kahoolawe, Maui, Lanai, Molokai, Oahu, Kauai, and Niihau. The islands stretch over 1,600 miles (2,574.88 kilometers). California is more than 2,000 miles (3,200 kilometers) away. Hawaii is the only state separated from North America.

Tourism is Hawaii's leading industry. Visitors enjoy the state's pleasant climate and beautiful beaches and mountains. Hawaii's ocean beaches have the big waves needed for surfboarding.

Hawaii's main products are pineapples and cane sugar. Other important crops are bananas, coffee, and nuts.

The Japanese attacked the naval base at Pearl Harbor on the island of Oahu. The attack took place on December 7, 1941. The U.S. declared war on Japan the next day. The U.S.S. *Arizona* Memorial is now located in Pearl Harbor.

## INTERESTING FACTS:

- Mt. Waialeale, on Kauai, receives more rain than any other spot on earth. It averages 460 inches (1,150 centimeters) of rain a year.
- The Haleakala Volcano has not been active since 1790. You can stay overnight in the crater in a rented cabin.
- The Silver Sword plant grows inside the Haleakala Volcano crater. It blooms only once in 20 years—then it dies.

# IDAHO

The name Idaho comes from the Shoshoni Indian words *ee-da-how*. That means "behold the sun coming down the mountain." Idaho has 22 different mountain ranges. There are also woodlands, areas like deserts, farmlands, lava wastelands, and beautiful lakes. Coeur d'Alene Lake is considered one of the world's prettiest.

The U.S. bought Idaho as part of the Louisiana Purchase. The area was explored by Meriwether Lewis and William Clark in 1805. An Indian woman, Sacajawea, and her husband were their guides.

The first permanent U.S. town in Idaho was Franklin. It was started by Mormons in 1860. That same year gold was discovered on Orofino Creek. Many prospectors came to Idaho searching for quick fortunes. When the gold ran out, the prospectors moved on. "Ghost towns" were left behind.

Mining is still important to this state. More than a third of all the silver mined in the U.S. comes from Idaho. Other minerals and gems like garnets are also mined here.

Idaho leads the states in potato production. Big Idaho potatoes are great for baking. Livestock, wheat, and other crops are also important products.

Tourists visit Idaho's lakes and streams for fishing, boating, and camping. The Sun Valley resort is popular for skiing and swimming. The state has eight national forests and parts of seven others.

**IDAHO (ID)**
**Capital:** Boise
**Flower:** Syringa (mock orange)
**Bird:** Mountain bluebird
**Tree:** White pine
**Nickname:** Gem State
**Admitted to Union:** July 3, 1890—43rd State
**Land Area:** 82,677 square miles (214,133 square kilometers)
**Total Area:** 83,557 square miles (216,412 square kilometers)
**1990 Population:** 1,006,749

Craters of the Moon National Monument is an interesting spot to visit. Its 80 square miles (207 square kilometers) look like the surface of the moon. Lava from ancient volcanoes formed many strange shapes.

**INTERESTING FACTS:**
- The deepest canyon in the U.S. is Hells Canyon. It divides Idaho from Oregon along the Snake River. The canyon is 1.5 miles (2.5 kilometers) deep.
- The largest elk herds in the U.S. are found in Idaho.
- The Fiddler's Hall of Fame is in Weiser. Every June fiddlers from all over North America have a contest there.

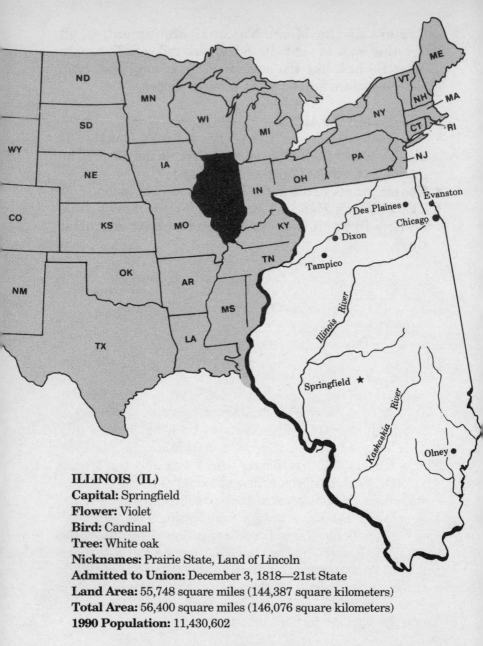

**ILLINOIS (IL)**
**Capital:** Springfield
**Flower:** Violet
**Bird:** Cardinal
**Tree:** White oak
**Nicknames:** Prairie State, Land of Lincoln
**Admitted to Union:** December 3, 1818—21st State
**Land Area:** 55,748 square miles (144,387 square kilometers)
**Total Area:** 56,400 square miles (146,076 square kilometers)
**1990 Population:** 11,430,602

# ILLINOIS

Chicago is the largest city in the state. It is also the third largest city in the U.S. O'Hare International Airport is the world's busiest. Chicago is the industrial center of the Midwest. It has a grain exchange, meat packers, iron and steel producers, and busy railroad centers. It is a major Great Lakes port.

In 1871 a terrible fire almost destroyed Chicago. A cow belonging to Mrs. O'Leary is blamed for starting the fire. The cow kicked over a lantern and the fire spread. The fire covered 3.5 square miles (9 square kilometers) and destroyed $200 billion worth of property. Several hundred people were killed.

In 1893 the World's Columbian Exposition was held in Chicago. It was an expensive and exciting world's fair. George Ferris invented a great new ride for the fair—the Ferris wheel. The first Ferris wheel was also the largest ever built. Each passenger car was as big as a bus.

Abraham Lincoln became the sixteenth president of the U.S. in 1860. He was a lawyer from Springfield. Today you can visit his home there. Lincoln was president during the Civil War. General Ulysses S. Grant helped the North win the Civil War. He was also from Illinois. Grant became the eighteenth president in 1869. President Ronald Reagan was born in Tampico, Illinois, and grew up in the town of Dixon. He was the fortieth president.

Illinois is a leader in manufacturing, coal mining, oil production, and agriculture. The state ranks second in hog production.

**INTERESTING FACTS:**
- The tallest building in the world is the Sears Tower in Chicago. It is 1,454 feet (443 meters) high.
- The first McDonald's restaurant in the world was built in Des Plaines in 1955.
- The town of Olney has more than 800 white squirrels. The squirrels are albinos.
- Ice cream sundaes were invented in Evanston by a soda fountain owner. Strict laws banned the selling of ice cream sodas on Sundays.

# INDIANA

There were many battles between Indians and settlers of Indiana in the 1700s and the early 1800s. In 1811, General William Henry Harrison won an important battle against the Shawnee Indians on the Tippecanoe River. He became known as Old Tippecanoe. William Henry Harrison became the ninth U.S. president in 1841. His grandson, Benjamin Harrison, became the twenty-third president in 1889.

Johnny Appleseed planted many trees in Indiana, Illinois, and Ohio in the early 1800s. He wore an old tin pot on his head for a hat and a coffee sack for a shirt. His real name was John Chapman. A Johnny Appleseed Festival is held in Fort Wayne every September.

Abraham Lincoln lived in Spencer County as a boy and young man. He lived in a log cabin and borrowed books to read. He and his family moved to Illinois when he was 21. You can visit a rebuilt log cabin like the one Lincoln lived in. It is near Lincoln City.

People from Indiana are called Hoosiers. Some people say the name came from pioneers calling out "Who's here?" Those words finally became the word Hoosier.

Every Memorial Day, car racing fans go to the Indianapolis Motor Speedway to watch the Indy 500. The 500-mile race is seen by more than 300,000 fans every year. The Indy 500 has taken place every year since 1911. It is the biggest single, spectator sport in the U.S.

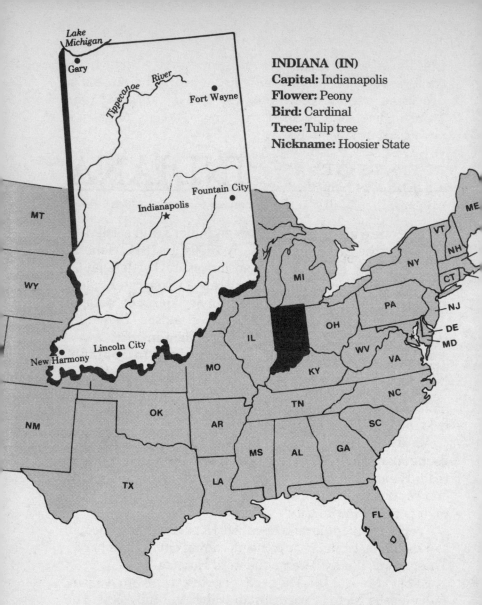

**INDIANA (IN)**
**Capital:** Indianapolis
**Flower:** Peony
**Bird:** Cardinal
**Tree:** Tulip tree
**Nickname:** Hoosier State

**Admitted to Union:** December 11, 1816—19th State
**Land Area:** 36,097 square miles (93,491 square kilometers)
**Total Area:** 36,291 square miles (93,993 square kilometers)
**1990 Population:** 5,544,159

Indiana is a leading state in agriculture. Corn, hogs, turkeys, soybeans, and grains are grown. The state also produces coal and limestone. The Lake Michigan waterfront is a major industrial area. The city of Gary is famous for its steel mills.

## INTERESTING FACTS:
- Levi Coffin helped over 2,000 slaves escape to Canada before the Civil War. His house in Fountain City was a main hiding place on the Underground Railroad.
- The first nursery school in the U.S. was started in New Harmony around 1825.
- James Whitcomb Riley was known as the Hoosier Poet. He wrote "Little Orphan Annie" and "The Raggedy Man."

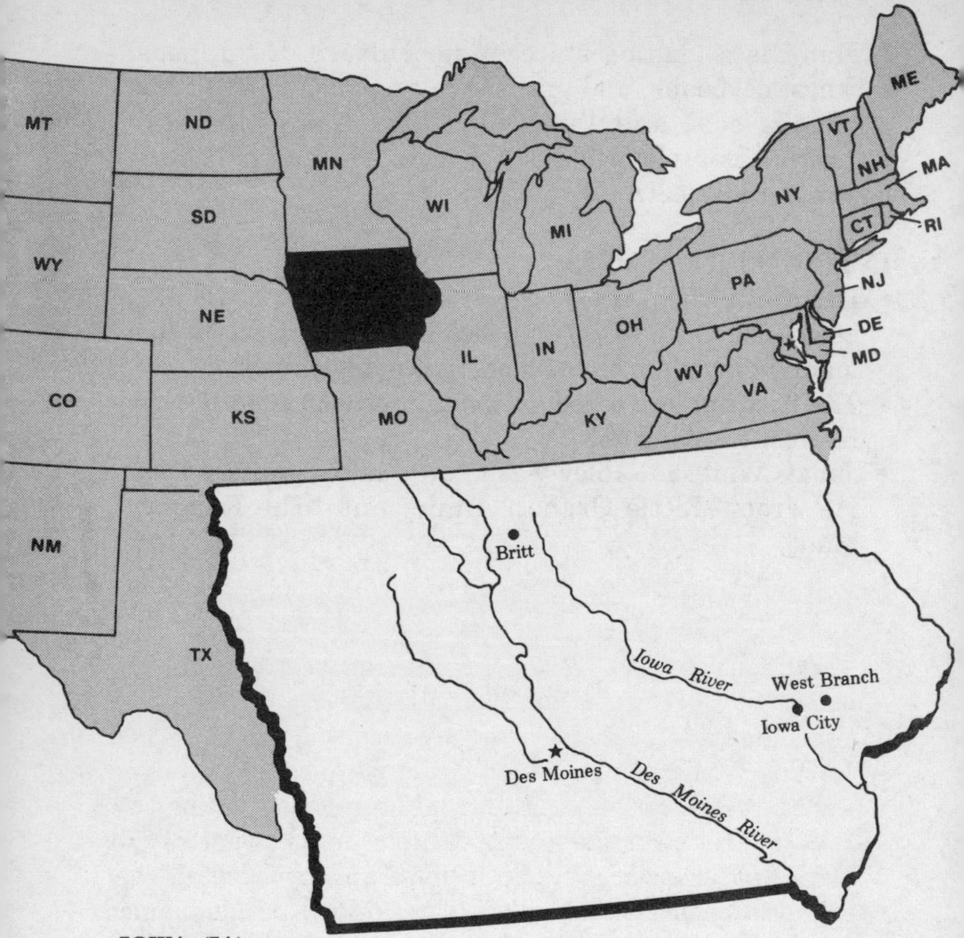

**IOWA (IA)**
**Capital:** Des Moines
**Flower:** Wild rose
**Bird:** Eastern goldfinch
**Tree:** Oak
**Nicknames:** Hawkeye State, Corn State
**Admitted to Union:** December 28, 1846—29th State
**Land Area:** 55,491 square miles (144,887 square kilometers)
**Total Area:** 56,290 square miles (145,790 square kilometers)
**1990 Population:** 2,776,755

# IOWA

Indians called Mound Builders built many earth mounds in Iowa long ago. Some mounds were used to bury the dead. Others were used as temples or forts. Some of the mounds were shaped like birds or animals.

This state's name came from the Ioway Indians. The name may be from an Algonquin Indian word meaning "beautiful land." Others think the name comes from an Indian word for "sleepy one."

William Cody's home state was Iowa. He became known as Buffalo Bill Cody in the mid 1800s because he was the greatest buffalo hunter on the prairies. He was also an Indian scout. His Wild West Show traveled all over the U.S. and Europe.

Herbert Hoover was the thirty-first president of the U.S. He was the first president from a state west of the Mississippi. Hoover grew up in Iowa and traveled all over the world before becoming president. Many people blamed him for the Great Depression of the 1930s. The Herbert Hoover Presidential Library is located in West Branch.

Iowa's black soil is some of the richest in the country. The soil and plenty of rain help produce fine crops. Iowa is the top agricultural state. It leads the U.S. in production of livestock, hogs, corn, and soybeans. Sometimes Iowa is called the "bread basket of the nation." Manufacturing, forestry, and mining are other major industries.

**INTERESTING FACTS:**
- The University of Iowa in Iowa City has one of the largest bagpipe bands in the world.
- The world's largest coffee pot is in Stanton. It is a modified water tower with a handle, spout, and painted flowers.
- A hobo convention is held every year in the town of Britt. A king and queen of the hoboes are elected.

# KANSAS

Kansas got its name from an Indian tribe of long ago. The tribe was the Kansa. The name meant "people of the south wind."

Many Kansas pioneers lived in sod houses because lumber was scarce. They cut blocks of prairie grass and used them like bricks. A recreated sod house is in Colby.

Dodge City was a famous frontier town of the Wild West. One street has been reconstructed to look like it did in the 1870s and 1880s.

Dwight Eisenhower grew up in Abilene with his four brothers. He became the thirty-fourth U.S. president. You can visit the home where he lived as a boy in Abilene. The Eisenhower Memorial Museum and Presidential Library are also located there.

Kansas is an important farming state. It leads the U.S. in the production of wheat. Along with Iowa, Kansas is known as the Breadbasket of America. The country's largest grain elevator is near Hutchinson. Kansas is also a leader in the production of helium, oil, and natural gas. Witchita leads the nation in the manufacturing of private airplanes.

Some of the best fossils have been found in Kansas. The largest beds of fossil crabs are found there. Kansas also has some unusual rock formations, like the Chalk Pyramids and Mushroom Rocks. Kansas is the geographical center of the forty-eight states (not including Alaska and Hawaii).

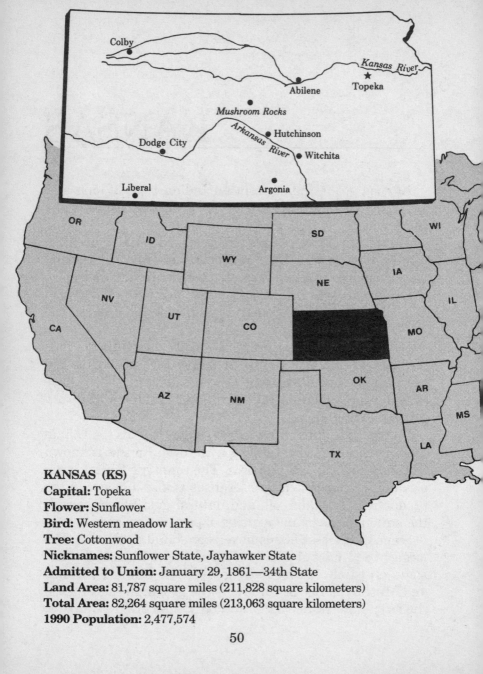

Colby

Kansas River

Abilene

★ Topeka

Mushroom Rocks

*Arkansas River*

Hutchinson

Dodge City

Witchita

Liberal

Argonia

OR
ID
WY
SD
WI
NV
NE
IA
UT
CO
IL
CA
MO
AZ
NM
OK
AR
MS
TX
LA

**KANSAS (KS)**
**Capital:** Topeka
**Flower:** Sunflower
**Bird:** Western meadow lark
**Tree:** Cottonwood
**Nicknames:** Sunflower State, Jayhawker State
**Admitted to Union:** January 29, 1861—34th State
**Land Area:** 81,787 square miles (211,828 square kilometers)
**Total Area:** 82,264 square miles (213,063 square kilometers)
**1990 Population:** 2,477,574

50

**INTERESTING FACTS:**
- The first woman mayor in the U.S. was Susanna Salter. She was elected in Argonia in 1887.
- The state animal is the buffalo. The state song is "Home on the Range."
- The International Pancake Race is held in Liberal every year. Runners have to carry a pancake in a skillet. They have to toss the pancake twice during race.

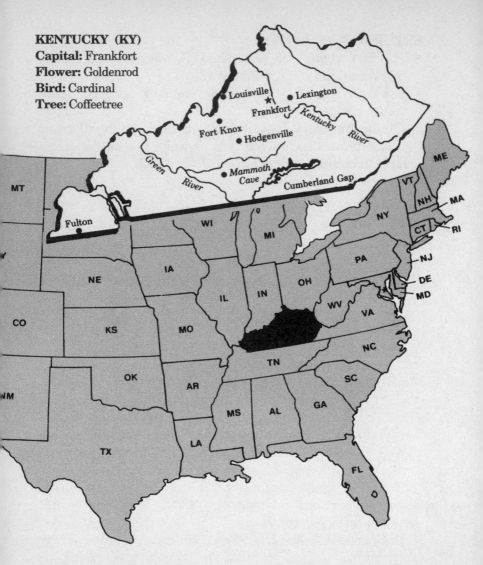

**KENTUCKY (KY)**
**Capital:** Frankfort
**Flower:** Goldenrod
**Bird:** Cardinal
**Tree:** Coffeetree

**Nickname:** Bluegrass State
**Admitted to Union:** June 1, 1792—15th State
**Land Area:** 39,650 square miles (102,694 square kilometers)
**Total Area:** 40,395 square miles (104,623 square kilometers)
**1990 Population:** 3,661,433

# KENTUCKY

Kentucky has more caves than any other state—more than 2,000. There are also probably more underground streams and rivers than in any other state. Kentucky has some of the best areas of fossils in the world. Fossils of mammoths, mastodons, and giant wolves have been found.

Mammoth Cave is one of the largest caves in the world. It has several underground rivers and lakes. A complete tour of the cave trails takes seven hours to complete.

Daniel Boone was one of the most famous explorers of the frontier. He was captured by Indians several times. Chief Black Fish adopted him as an honorary son. Boone and his men built the Wilderness Road through the Cumberland Gap and began Fort Boonesborough in 1775.

Abraham Lincoln was born in a log cabin in Hardin County in 1809. His family moved to Indiana when he was seven. You can visit the original log cabin near Hodgenville.

Kentucky was a border state during the Civil War. The state was part of the Union (the North), but many people were on the side of the South.

Lexington is called the Horse Center of America. There are hundreds of horse farms in the state. Kentucky is known as the Bluegrass State because the grass of the horse farms has a blue-green tint when blossoms appear in the spring.

The Kentucky Derby is run every year in May at

Churchill Downs in Louisville. The "Run for the Roses" is the oldest horse race in the U.S. It was first run in 1875.

Kentucky is first in the U.S. in production of bituminous coal and burley tobacco. In pioneer days tobacco could be used as money. Kentucky is also a leader in dairy products, oil, clay, and forestry.

## INTERESTING FACTS:
- The U.S. gold reserves are stored at Fort Knox. The door to the vault weighs 20 tons.
- The Hatfield and McCoy families started feuding (fighting) in 1882 over a fifty-cent debt for a fiddle. The feud went on for years and more than 100 people were killed.
- The International Banana Festival is held every September in the towns of Fulton, Kentucky, and South Fulton, Tennessee. The world's largest banana pudding is cooked and visitors are given free bananas.

# LOUISIANA

Louisiana was owned by France and Spain in the 1700s. It became part of the U.S. with the Louisiana Purchase. Louisiana is called the Gateway to the Mississippi Valley. Part of the state was formed by soil carried down the river. This area is called the Delta. There are many levees (concrete walls) to keep the river from flooding.

The Battle of New Orleans was fought in 1815 between the U.S. and the British. General Andrew Jackson led the U.S. troops. He became the seventh U.S. president.

Jean Lafitte (sometimes spelled Laffite) was a New Orleans blacksmith who became a famous pirate and smuggler. He was a folk hero to many people. Lafitte and his men helped General Jackson in the Battle of New Orleans. They were pardoned by President James Madison. The town of Lafitte is named for the famous pirate.

New Orleans is Louisiana's most famous city. Tourists love visiting the French Quarter, with its famous restaurants and old buildings. Mardi Gras is a carnival held every year before Lent. There are parades, parties, music, and fancy balls. Jazz music had its start in New Orleans. It is the only truly American form of music.

The Louisiana Superdome in New Orleans is the largest enclosed stadium in history. It is the world's largest steel-constructed room. Up to 95,000 people can view events in the main arena.

**LOUISIANA (LA)**
**Capital:** Baton Rouge
**Flower:** Magnolia
**Bird:** Pelican
**Tree:** Bald cypress
**Nickname:** Pelican State

**Admitted to Union:** April 30, 1812—18th State
**Land Area:** 44,930 square miles (116,369 square kilometers)
**Total Area:** 48,523 square miles (125,674 square kilometers)
**1990 Population:** 4,219,973

New Orleans, Baton Rouge, and Lake Charles are all deep-water ports important in shipping. Louisiana is a leader in oil products, sweet potatoes, rice, cotton, soybeans, sugarcane, and furs.

## INTERESTING FACTS:

- The capital city, Baton Rouge, got its name in an unusual way. *Baton Rouge* means "red stick" in French. Indians had marked the site of the town with a red tree trunk.
- The flags of France, Spain, England, West Florida, the Louisiana Republic, and the United States have flown over Baton Rouge.
- The first apartments in the U.S. are the Pontalba Apartments. They are located in the French Quarter of New Orleans. They were built from 1849 to 1851 by the Baroness Pontalba.

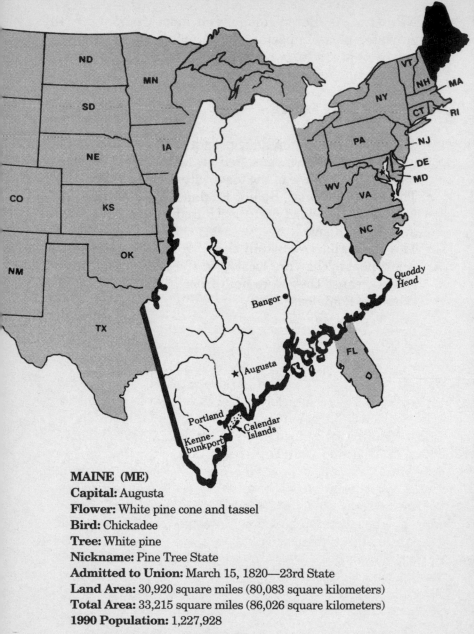

**MAINE (ME)**
**Capital:** Augusta
**Flower:** White pine cone and tassel
**Bird:** Chickadee
**Tree:** White pine
**Nickname:** Pine Tree State
**Admitted to Union:** March 15, 1820—23rd State
**Land Area:** 30,920 square miles (80,083 square kilometers)
**Total Area:** 33,215 square miles (86,026 square kilometers)
**1990 Population:** 1,227,928

# MAINE

The most eastern point in the continental U.S. is West Quoddy Head. Maine is the only state with just one other state—New Hampshire—on its boundary. Its other boundaries are Canada and the Atlantic Ocean.

Maine's coastline has rocky cliffs, lighthouses, sandy beaches, and many bays and islands. Tourists enjoy visiting fishing villages and eating Maine lobster. The state also has large forests and beautiful mountains. There are more than 5,000 rivers and streams and more than 6,000 lakes.

The Calendar Islands are in Casco Bay off Portland. They got their name because there are as many islands as days in the year. There are many legends about buried pirate treasure on the islands. Captain Kidd is thought to have buried his loot on Jewell Island. The islands have interesting names: for example, Littlejohn, Whaleboat, Pumpkin Nob, and Pound of Tea.

Maine was part of Massachusetts before becoming a state. People from Massachusetts traveled northeast to get to Maine. They said they were going "down east." *Down* may have meant *north* long ago. People from Maine have been called Down Easters ever since.

One of America's most famous poets was from Maine. Henry Wadsworth Longfellow was born in Portland and attended Bowdoin College. He wrote *The Song of Hiawatha,* a famous long poem about Indians, in 1855.

Maine is a leader in wood products, lobster, sardines, and blueberries. Ships have been built in Maine since the 1600s.

**INTERESTING FACTS:**

- Maine and Canada fought the Aroostook War from 1838 to 1839. They were fighting over their boundary. No shots were fired.
- National Dump Week is celebrated in Kennebunkport every July. There is a beauty contest to select Miss Dumpy.
- In Bangor there is a statue of Paul Bunyan that is 31 feet (9.4 meters) tall. "Tall tales" are told about Paul Bunyan all through the northern states.

# MARYLAND

In 1608 Captain John Smith visited the Chesapeake Bay area. England granted a colonial charter to Lord Baltimore in 1632.

Maryland got its nickname of the Old Line State during the Revolutionary War. A group of soldiers was called the Maryland Line. They held back the British Army while General George Washington withdrew to Manhattan Island. Baltimore was the only major port not captured by the British during the Revolutionary War.

Annapolis served as the nation's capital for eight months from 1783 to 1784. The U.S. Naval Academy is located there.

Francis Scott Key wrote the words of "The Star Spangled Banner" during the War of 1812. He was a young lawyer from Frederick. During a battle he waited until dawn to see which flag was flying over Fort McHenry in Baltimore.

The oldest Navy ship still afloat is the U.S. frigate *Constellation*. It was launched in 1797. You can visit it in Baltimore Harbor.

Edgar Allen Poe was a famous writer from Baltimore. He wrote many scary stories.

The Chesapeake Bay almost splits the state in two. The bay produces excellent seafood. The long coastline helps make Maryland a leader in shipping and fishing. Tobacco, vegetable canning, and manufacturing are also important to the state's economy.

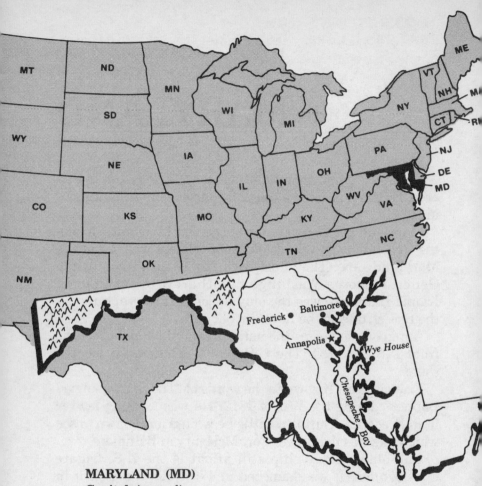

**MARYLAND (MD)**
**Capital:** Annapolis
**Flower:** Black-eyed Susan
**Bird:** Baltimore oriole
**Tree:** White oak
**Nickname:** Old Line State, Free State
**Admitted to Union:** April 28, 1788—7th State
**Land Area:** 9,891 square miles (25,618 square kilometers)
**Total Area:** 10,577 square miles (27,394 square kilometers)
**1990 Population:** 4,781,468

## INTERESTING FACTS:

- The largest white oak tree in the U.S. is at Wye House, a historic home.
- Maryland is the only state with an official state dog, the Chesapeake Bay retriever.
- The complete fossil of a whale was found at Calvert Cliffs. Fossils from these cliffs have been studied since the 1600s .

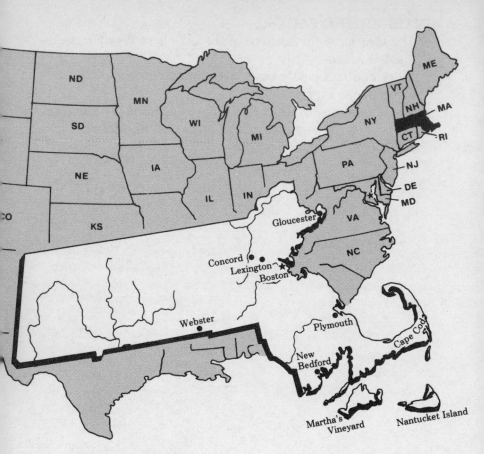

**MASSACHUSETTS (MA)**
**Capital:** Boston
**Flower:** Mayflower
**Bird:** Chickadee
**Tree:** American elm
**Nicknames:** Bay State, Old Colony State
**Admitted to Union:** February 6, 1788—6th State
**Land Area:** 7,826 square miles (20,269 square kilometers)
**Total Area:** 8,257 square miles (21,385 square kilometers)
**1990 Population:** 6,016,425

# MASSACHUSETTS

This state has played an important part in U.S. history. The Pilgrims founded Plymouth Colony in 1620. A copy of their ship, the *Mayflower,* is at Plymouth today.

Massachusetts was a leader in the events that led to the Revolutionary War. In 1773 the Boston Tea Party took place in Boston Harbor. Patriots dressed like Indians dumped tea into the harbor. They were protesting a tax on tea. Paul Revere made his famous ride in 1775 to warn of the coming British army. At Concord and Lexington early battles were fought. The Battle of Bunker Hill was the first major battle of the war. It was actually fought on Breed's Hill in Boston.

Five presidents were from Massachusetts. John Adams and John Quincy Adams were the only father and son to both become president. Calvin Coolidge and John F. Kennedy were also from Massachusetts. George Bush, the 41st president, was born in Milton.

The oldest college in the U.S. is Harvard University in Boston. It was started in 1636. Another historic sight in Boston is the U.S.S. *Constitution.* It is also known as Old Ironsides.

The sea has always been important to Massachusetts. Martha's Vineyard, Nantucket Island, and New Bedford were important whaling ports. Gloucester is still an important fishing town. Cape Cod is a favorite vacation spot for many tourists.

The official state beverage is cranberry juice. Massachusetts produces more cranberries than any other state. Electronics, communications equipment, and tourism are important industries.

**INTERESTING FACTS:**
- Louisa May Alcott lived in Concord in the 1800s. She wrote *Little Women* and *Little Men*.
- The lake with the world's longest name is in Webster. The name is Lake Chargoggagoggmanchauggauggagoggchaubunagungamau. It was named by the Nipmuc Indians. The name means, " I fish on my side; you fish on your side; and no one fishes in the middle."
- Many people believe that the real Mother Goose lived in Boston in the 1600s. Her name was Mrs. Mary Goose. She wrote nursery rhymes for her grandchildren.

# MICHIGAN

French explorers traveled through Michigan in the 1600s. The first permanent settlement was Sault Sainte Marie (pronounced Soo Saint Marie). Father Marquette founded it in 1668. Fort Mackinac (pronounced Mackinaw) and Fort Michilimackinac were important outposts in the settling of the Great Lakes region. Whoever controlled the Straits of Mackinac also controlled the Great Lakes.

Michigan is the only state made up of two peninsulas. The Upper Peninsula and the Lower Peninsula are joined by the Mackinac Bridge. It is one of the world's longest suspension bridges. Michigan is the only state bordering on four of the five Great Lakes—Michigan, Superior, Huron, and Erie. (The other Great Lake is Ontario.) Shipping on the Great Lakes helped make Michigan an industrial state.

The Tulip Time Festival has been held in the town of Holland every spring for over 50 years. The streets are scrubbed for parades and wooden-shoe dancers. Millions of tulips are in bloom for the festival.

Detroit is known as the Motor City. The U.S. automobile industry is centered here. Henry Ford was the leading pioneer of the auto industry. The Henry Ford Museum and Greenfield Village in Dearborn have many old cars, restored homes, and famous buildings. You can see the Wright brothers' cycle shop and Thomas Edison's laboratory.

**MICHIGAN (MI)**
**Capital:** Lansing
**Flower:** Apple blossom
**Bird:** Robin
**Tree:** White pine
**Nicknames:** Water Wonderland, Wolverine State
**Admitted to Union:** January 26, 1837—26th State
**Land Area:** 56,817 square miles (147,156 square kilometers)
**Total Area:** 58,216 square miles (150,779 square kilometers)
**1990 Population:** 9,295,297

Michigan is the leading producer of automobiles, red tart cherries, navy beans, pickle cucumbers, winter wheat, and Christmas trees. Cereals and furniture are other major industries. Tourists enjoy more than 11,000 inland lakes, the beaches of the Great Lakes, and many ski areas.

**INTERESTING FACTS:**
- The Grand Hotel on Mackinac Island has the world's longest front porch. No cars are allowed on the island.
- Telephone customers in Detroit were assigned the first telephone numbers in the U.S. in 1879.
- The thirty-eighth president was Gerald Ford. He grew up in Grand Rapids.

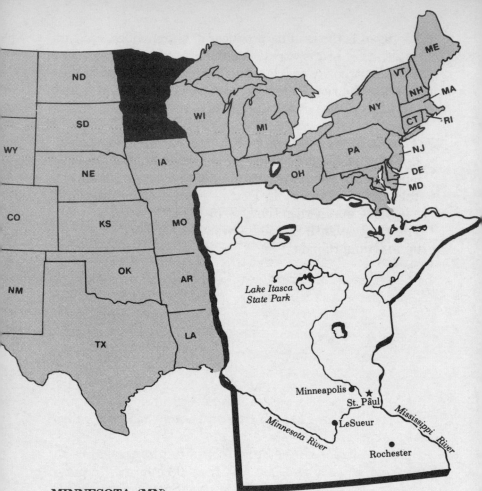

**MINNESOTA (MN)**
**Capital:** St. Paul
**Flower:** Pink and white lady's-slipper
**Bird:** Common loon
**Tree:** Red or Norway pine
**Nicknames:** North Star State, Gopher State
**Admitted to Union:** May 11, 1858—32nd State
**Land Area:** 79,289 square miles (205,359 square kilometers)
**Total Area:** 84,068 square miles (217,735 square kilometers)
**1990 Population:** 4,375,099

# MINNESOTA

The name Minnesota comes from Indian words for "sky-tinted water." The state is often called the Land of Sky-Blue Waters. Minneapolis is the state's largest city. Its name comes from the Indian word *minnehaha*, meaning "laughing water," and the Greek word *polis*, meaning "city."

Minneapolis and St. Paul are called the Twin Cities. The Mississippi River separates them. A small creek in Lake Itasca State Park is the beginning of the mighty Mississippi River. The Mississippi River is the longest river in the U.S.

The Mayo Clinic is located in Rochester. It is one of the most famous medical research centers in the world. Dr. William Mayo moved to Minnesota in 1855. His two sons, William and Charles, became doctors too. The Mayo family organized the clinic in 1889.

Some people believe that Norse explorers came to Minnesota as early as 1,000 A.D. In 1898 a farmer found a strange stone under the roots of a tree. Some experts think the markings on the stone were Norse words. They believe the Norsemen left the stone in 1362. Other people believe the stone is a fake.

Minnesota leads the U.S. in iron ore production. Grains, sugar beets, wild rice, and dairy products are important in the state's agriculture. St. Paul is the leading U.S. producer of calendars and law books. The state has over 15,000 lakes used for fishing and water sports.

## INTERESTING FACTS:

- Scotch Tape was invented by the Minnesota Mining and Manufacturing Company (3M).
- Minnesota has 91 Long Lakes, 76 Mud Lakes, 43 Rice Lakes, and 40 Twin Lakes.
- There is a huge statue of the Jolly Green Giant in LeSueur. The town has a Corn-on-the-Curb Celebration every year.

# MISSISSIPPI

The first permanent settlement in Mississippi was started in 1699 by a French group. It was near where Biloxi is today. The state later belonged to France and Spain. It became a part of the U.S. in 1810.

The Mississippi River has always been important to the state. Steam boats used to take passengers up and down the river. Barges and flatboats have long been used for shipping manufactured goods and crops.

During the Civil War the Union wanted to control the river. That way the South would be split in two. The Union finally captured Vicksburg in 1863. The port of Vicksburg controlled the river traffic.

Shipping is still important to the state today. The main ports are Pascagoula and Vicksburg. Atomic submarines are built at Pascagoula.

Jefferson Davis was a planter and U.S. Congressman from Mississippi. He became the president of the Confederacy. William Faulkner was a famous writer from the small town of Oxford. He wrote many stories about Southern life.

Mississippi is also an agricultural state. Cotton, soybeans, catfish, and rice, are the main crops. Manufacturing has increased in the last 20 years. Forestry and oil products are also important industries. Tourists can visit many old Southern mansions and sandy beaches on the Gulf of Mexico.

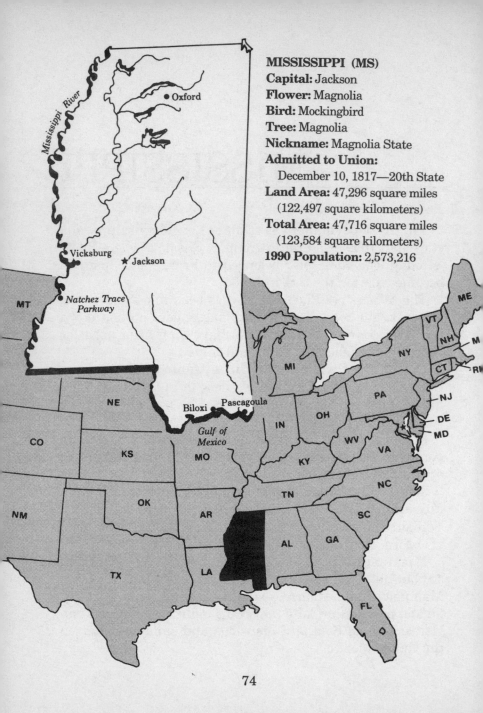

**MISSISSIPPI (MS)**
**Capital:** Jackson
**Flower:** Magnolia
**Bird:** Mockingbird
**Tree:** Magnolia
**Nickname:** Magnolia State
**Admitted to Union:**
   December 10, 1817—20th State
**Land Area:** 47,296 square miles
   (122,497 square kilometers)
**Total Area:** 47,716 square miles
   (123,584 square kilometers)
**1990 Population:** 2,573,216

**INTERESTING FACTS:**

- The old Biloxi Lighthouse was built in 1848. A mother and daughter served as lighthouse keepers for 62 years. Their names were Maria and Miranda Younghans. The lighthouse is now automatic.
- The state's schoolchildren chose the magnolia as the state flower in 1900. Mississippi is the only state with the official state flower from the state tree.
- The Natchez Trace was a path used by buffalo, Indians, and later by explorers and pioneers. Today it is a highway called the Natchez Trace Parkway.

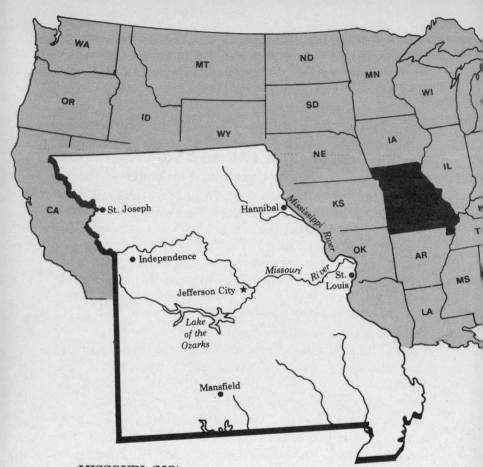

**MISSOURI (MO)**
**Capital:** Jefferson City
**Flower:** Hawthorn
**Bird:** Bluebird
**Tree:** Dogwood
**Nickname:** Show Me State
**Admitted to Union:** August 10, 1821—24th State
**Land Area:** 68,995 square miles (178,697 square kilometers)
**Total Area:** 69,686 square miles (180,486 square kilometers)
**1990 Population:** 5,117,073

# MISSOURI

Missouri is often called the Gateway to the West. Many pioneers passed through the state on their way west. The Sante Fe Trail and the Oregon Trail both began at Independence. Pony Express riders carried the mail from St. Joseph to California.The tallest monument in the U.S. is the Gateway Arch in St. Louis. It was built in 1966. It looks like a huge rainbow of steel. You can ride to the top in an elevator and look out from an observation deck.

The Mississippi River forms the eastern border of the state. The Missouri River cuts across the state. One of the largest man-made lakes in the world is the Lake of the Ozarks. It is created by the Bagnell Dam.

A little boy named Samuel Clemens grew up in Hannibal. He later became a riverboat pilot on the Mississippi River. He used the name Mark Twain when he became a writer. *Tom Sawyer* and *Huckleberry Finn* are based on his boyhood in Missouri.

Harry S. Truman was the thirty-third president. He was from Independence. The Harry S. Truman Library in Independence was the first presidential library. It has more than ten million of Truman's papers and documents.

St. Louis is an important transportation center. Missouri leads the world in production of lead. The state also produces soybeans, corn, cotton, beer, barite, and other minerals.

**INTERESTING FACTS:**

- Jesse James was a famous outlaw from Missouri. A $10,000 reward was offered for his capture. He was killed in 1882.
- Laura Ingalls Wilder and her husband, Almanzol, lived on a farm near Mansfield. She wrote the Little House books there.
- Life-size statues of Tom Sawyer and Huckleberry Finn can be seen in Hannibal. The National Fence Painting Contest is also held there every year.

# MONTANA

Many dinosaur fossils have been found in Montana. A tyrannosaurus rex was found near Jordan. A complete triceratops was found near Glendive. A relative of the horned toad called a hoplitosaurus was found near Billings. It was 15 feet (4.6 meters) tall!

One of the most famous battles in U.S. history was the Battle of Little Big Horn in 1876. General Custer and his 264 men were killed by Sioux and Cheyenne Indians. The only survivor of Custer's forces was a horse named Comanche. The battle is also called Custer's Last Stand.

The last major Indian battle in Montana was in 1877. At the Battle of the Bear's Paw, Chief Joseph surrendered. He said, "I will fight no more, forever."

Glacier National Park is in northwest Montana on the boundary between the U.S. and Canada. There are over 50 glaciers in the Rocky Mountains in this park. The largest glacier in the park covers about three square miles.

Billings is Montana's largest city. Virginia City is a restored mining town. Over $300 million in gold was mined there between 1863 and 1937. Butte is said to be the richest hill in the world. It was once an important copper mining center.

Montana is called the Treasure State for its rich natural resources. There were several gold strikes in the 1860s. Silver was mined next and copper followed that. Today

**MONTANA (MT)**
**Capital:** Helena
**Flower:** Bitterroot
**Bird:** Western meadow lark
**Tree:** Ponderosa pine
**Nickname:** Treasure State
**Admitted to Union:** November 8, 1889—41st State
**Land Area:** 145,587 square miles (377,070 square kilometers)
**Total Area:** 147,138 square miles (381,086 square kilometers)
**1990 Population:** 799,065

sapphires and many other precious and semiprecious stones are found in the state. Montana has huge reserves of coal and oil. The state is a leader in wheat, barley, sheep, cattle, copper, and oil. There are many large farms and ranches. Tourists can visit dude ranches.

**INTERESTING FACTS:**
- Charles M. Russell was one of the most famous artists of the West. He was a sheepherder and cowboy before becoming an artist in the late 1800s.
- In 1917 Jeannette Rankin became the first woman elected to the U.S. Congress. She was from Missoula.
- Some of the state's rivers have unusual names: Milk, Flathead, Rosebud, Tongue, Powder, Blackfoot, and Big Horn.

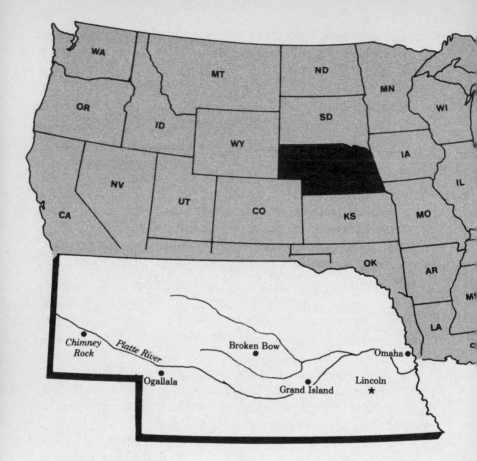

**NEBRASKA (NE)**
**Capital:** Lincoln
**Flower:** Goldenrod
**Bird:** Western meadow lark
**Tree:** Cottonwood
**Nickname:** Cornhusker State
**Admitted to Union:** March 1, 1867—37st State
**Land Area:** 76,483 square miles (198,091 square kilometers)
**Total Area:** 77,227 square miles (200,017 square kilometers)
**1990 Population:** 1,578,385

# NEBRASKA

Many pioneers passed through Nebraska on the way to the far West. Nebraska became a territory in 1854 and settlers began to stay. The Homestead Act in 1862 allowed people to claim up to 160 acres (65 hectares) of land. They had to live on it and farm it for five years. Then they would own the land. The first homestead claim in the U.S. was filed in Nebraska.

There were very few trees when Nebraska was being settled. The pioneers planted more than two million trees. In 1872 Arbor Day became a holiday to praise the trees and to plant new ones.

There were many Indian battles as Nebraska was settled. The Indians fought to protect their home lands. The government moved the Nebraska Indians to reservations in Oklahoma. The Indian wars ended after 1877.

At the Stuhr Museum and Land of the Prairie Pioneer near Grand Island, you can see how Nebraska pioneers lived. There are over 50 buildings from the 1800s. They include a Pawnee Indian village, a farm, and a pioneer village.

There have been five capitol buildings in Nebraska. There were two territorial capitols in Omaha and three state capitols in Lincoln. The present capitol was built slowly from 1922 to 1932. The state continued building whenever there was enough money.

Nebraska's state legislature is different from all the other states. Nebraska's legislature is unicameral. That means there is only one elected chamber, called the Senate. Other states have two chambers: the Senate and the House.

Nebraska is a leading grain state. Rye, corn, and wheat are the biggest crops. Cattle and hogs are raised throughout the state. Omaha is the largest meat-packing center in the U.S. It is also the largest city in Nebraska.

## INTERESTING FACTS:

- Ogallala was one of Nebraska's frontier towns of the Old West. Today Front Street is restored and shoot-outs are staged for visitors.
- The town of Broken Bow was named after a broken Indian bow. The only two-story sod house still standing in the U.S. is there.
- Chimney Rock is a tall piece of sandstone that was a famous landmark to the pioneers. It rises 350 feet (107 meters) above the Platte River.
- Buffalo Bill Cody's home and memorabilia of his Wild West Show can be seen at the Buffalo Bill Ranch State Historical Park in North Platte.

# NEVADA

Gold was discovered in Nevada as early as 1847. The early gold prospectors had trouble mining the gold because of blue clay that stuck to it. That blue clay turned out to be almost pure silver!

Thousands of fortune seekers moved to Nevada in 1859 and 1860. The best silver mining area became known as the Comstock Lode. Copper, lead, zinc, and other minerals were mined in addition to gold and silver. Large silver deposits were discovered in the early 1900s at Tonopah and Goldfield.

Virginia City was one of the most important towns of the Old West. Mark Twain got his start as a writer there for a newspaper, *The Territorial Enterprise*. The streets of Virginia City were said to be paved with silver. Discarded low-grade ore from the mines was used. Today the town is restored and there are many buildings open to tourists.

Las Vegas is called the Entertainment and Gambling Capital of the World. Gambling is legal in the state of Nevada. About 12 million people a year visit Las Vegas. There are many shows in the big hotels featuring top stars.

Lake Mead is one of the largest man-made lakes. The Sahara Cup Races for hydroplanes are held there every year. The lake is created by the Hoover Dam. The dam is as high as a 44-story building. It provides electricity and irrigation.

Today Nevada mines produce copper, gold, titanium, mercury, sulphur, and many other minerals. Most of the

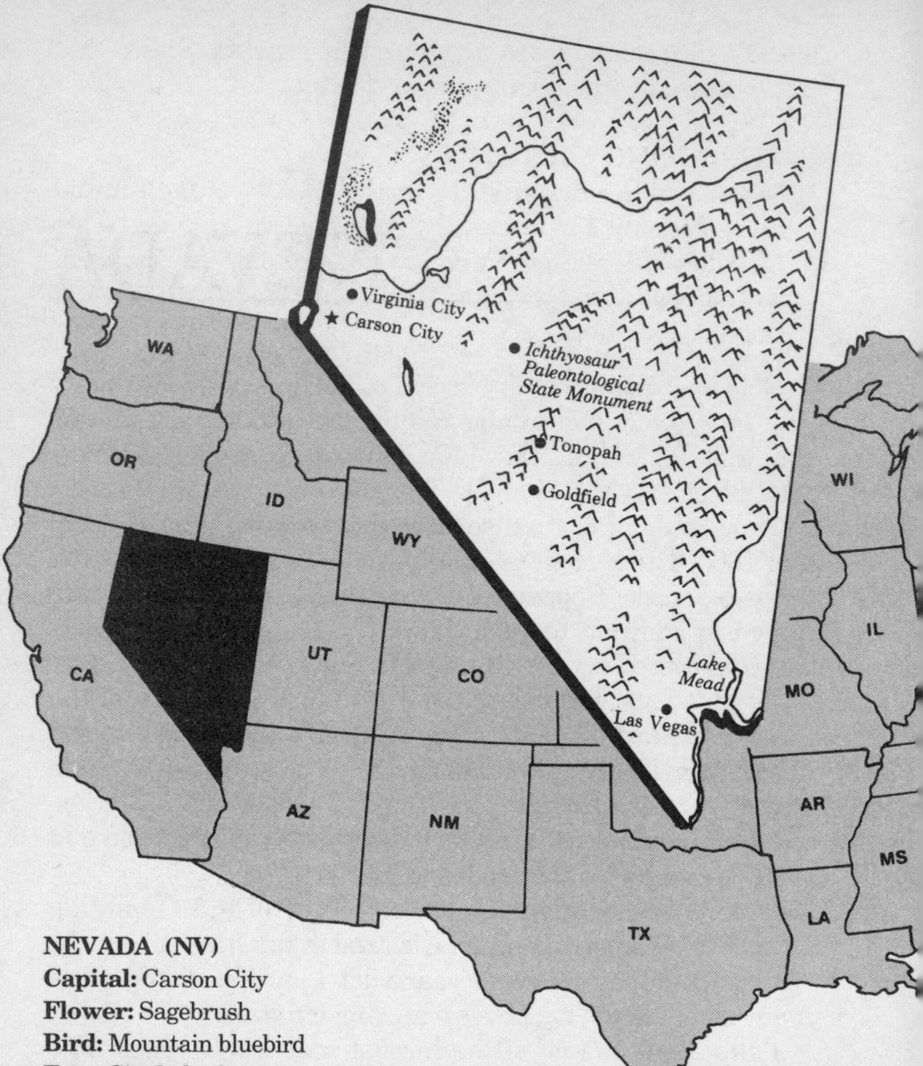

**NEVADA (NV)**
**Capital:** Carson City
**Flower:** Sagebrush
**Bird:** Mountain bluebird
**Tree:** Single-leaf piñon
**Nicknames:** Silver State, Sagebrush State
**Admitted to Union:** October 31, 1864—36th State
**Land Area:** 109,889 square miles (284,613 square kilometers)
**Total Area:** 110,540 square miles (286,297 square kilometers)
**1990 Population:** 1,201,833

world's turquoise stones are found in Nevada. Sheep and cattle ranching are important in agriculture.

**INTERESTING FACTS:**
- Nevada is the driest state in the U.S. Average annual rainfall is only 3.73 inches (9.47 centimeters).
- At Valley of Fire State Park you can see some unusual rock formations. Two of the most famous are Elephant Rock and Donald Duck Rock.
- Ichthyosaur Paleontological State Monument is in Nye County. There are many fossils of huge prehistoric fish-reptiles called ichthyosaurs.

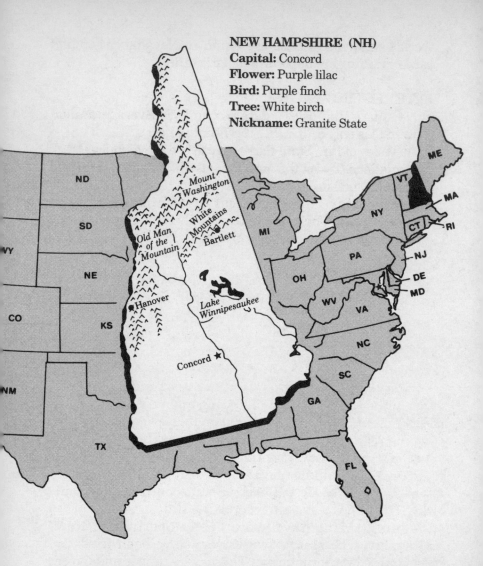

**NEW HAMPSHIRE (NH)**
**Capital:** Concord
**Flower:** Purple lilac
**Bird:** Purple finch
**Tree:** White birch
**Nickname:** Granite State

**Admitted to Union:** June 21, 1788—9th State
**Land Area:** 9,027 square miles (23,380 square kilometers)
**Total Area:** 9,304 square miles (24,097 square kilometers)
**1990 Population:** 1,109,252

# NEW HAMPSHIRE

The highest mountain in the northeast U.S. is Mount Washington. It is 6,288 feet (1,917 meters) high. Mount Washington is part of the Presidential Range of the White Mountains.

The Old Man of the Mountain is a profile of a bearded man at the top of a cliff. The face is made of several granite ledges that stick out from the cliff. This natural monument overlooks Franconia Notch. It is the state's official emblem.

Beautiful forests cover most of the state. There are many maples and other trees that have bright fall colors. Tourism is an important industry in the state.

New Hampshire was one of the 13 original states. But no Revolutionary War battles were fought there. New Hampshire was the ninth state to ratify the U.S. Constitution in 1788. That vote put the new Constitution into effect.

President Franklin Pierce was born in a log cabin in New Hampshire. He became the fourteenth president in 1853. His father was a governor of the state.

Manufacturing has always been important in New Hampshire.The state's swift rivers have been used for providing power for industry. There were timber and paper mills in the state in the 1600s and 1700s. Shipbuilding, textiles, maple products, leather goods, and machinery are major products. Dairying and poultry are most important in agriculture.

## INTERESTING FACTS:

- The Dartmouth Winter Carnival is held every year at Dartmouth College in Hanover. Huge statues and sculptures are carved out of ice. Some are 30 feet (9 meters) tall.
- The world's longest slide is on a hill near Bartlett. It is three-fourths of a mile (1.21 kilometers) long.
- Lake Winnipesaukee is the state's largest lake. Over the years the name was spelled more than 130 different ways. The state legislature made the spelling official in 1931.

# NEW JERSEY

New Jersey is called the Crossroads of the East. There are more than 15,000 factories in the state. Chemicals, oil products, glass, clothing, and machinery are some of the state's products. Food processing is also important. The Campbell Company in Camden started canning soup in 1869. The town is famous for its pleasant smell of cooking tomatoes and spices. There are over 600 research laboratories in the state.

One of the most famous paintings in U.S. history shows a Revolutionary War scene. George Washington and his men crossed the Delaware River on Christmas night in 1776. In Trenton, Washington's troops surprised the British and their hired German soldiers and won the battle. Many other Revolutionary War battles were fought in New Jersey.

Thomas Edison had two of the country's first research laboratories in Menlo Park and West Orange. He invented the electric light bulb and the phonograph and improved motion pictures. He was called the Wizard of Menlo Park. Samuel Morse invented the telegraph in Morristown.

Grover Cleveland was born in Caldwell. He became the twenty-second U.S. president in 1885. He lost the next election. In 1892 he was reelected and became the twenty-fourth U.S. president.

Woodrow Wilson was a college teacher who became president of Princeton College. He went on to become the

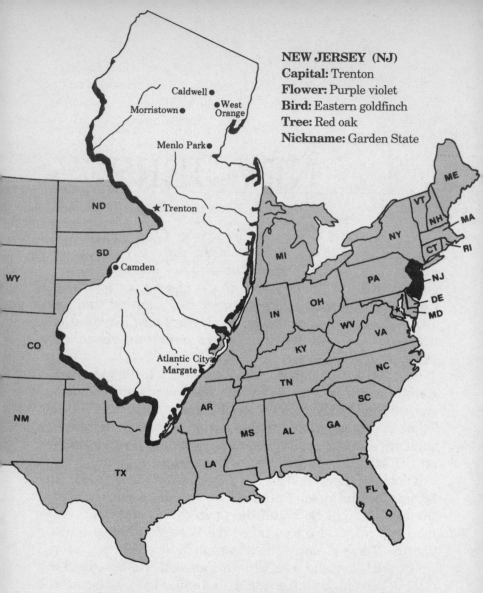

**NEW JERSEY (NJ)**
**Capital:** Trenton
**Flower:** Purple violet
**Bird:** Eastern goldfinch
**Tree:** Red oak
**Nickname:** Garden State

**Admitted to Union:** December 18, 1787—3rd State
**Land Area:** 7,521 square miles (19,479 square kilometers)
**Total Area:** 7,836 square miles (20,295 square kilometers)
**1990 Population:** 7,730,188

governor of New Jersey. In 1913 he became the twenty-eighth U.S. president. He was president during World War I.

Atlantic City is famous for its long boardwalk, beach hotels, and gambling casinos. The Miss America Pageant is held there every year.

## INTERESTING FACTS:

- A Swedish colony was started in 1638 in what is now New Jersey. In 1643 Johan Printz became its governor. He was seven feet (two meters) tall and weighed 400 pounds (181 kilograms). The Indians called him Big Tub.
- The property cards in the board game Monopoly are named after streets in Atlantic City.
- In the town of Margate is a huge statue of an elephant named Lucy. It is 75 feet (25.9 meters) tall and was built in 1883.

**NEW MEXICO (NM)**

**Capital:** Santa Fe

**Flower:** Yucca

**Bird:** Roadrunner

**Tree:** Piñon (nut pine)

**Nickname:** Land of Enchantment

**Admitted to Union:** January 6, 1912—47th State

**Land Area:** 121,412 square miles (314,457 square kilometers)

**Total Area:** 121,666 square miles (315,113 square kilometers)

**1990 Population:** 1,515,069

# NEW MEXICO

Carlsbad Caverns are some of the world's largest. You can take a four-hour guided tour and eat lunch underground. There is also an elevator down to the caverns. Five kinds of bats live in the caves.

Indians have lived in New Mexico for thousands of years. The Pueblo Indians built houses like apartments. The houses are called pueblos, too. Some had hundreds of rooms for over a thousand people. Other Indians of the state are the Navahos, Apaches, Utes, Zunis, and Comanches.

The Indians of New Mexico are famous for their crafts. Pottery, silver and turquoise jewelry, weavings, and paintings are bought by visitors to the state.

Spanish culture has also been important to the history of New Mexico. Explorers from Spain came to New Mexico looking for gold. Missionaries followed to work with the Indians. Spain and Mexico controlled the area for many years. Today Spanish and English are both official state languages.

New Mexico is a leader in energy research, uranium, potassium, and oil products. Livestock, cotton, and wheat are also important. Tourism is one of the state's major industries. Visitors enjoy the pleasant weather and pretty scenery. New Mexico has mountains, deserts, forests, lakes, and canyons.

Santa Fe is the oldest state capital. It was founded in 1610. Its capitol building is the only round one in the nation.

**INTERESTING FACTS:**

- The oldest highway in the U.S. is El Camino Real ("the King's Highway"). The road runs from Santa Fe to Mexico City. Spanish travelers used this road in 1581 .
- Billy the Kid was a young outlaw in frontier days. He escaped from the Lincoln County Courthouse after killing two guards. There is a frontier museum in Lincoln.
- Every December the Zuni Indians have a special ceremony called the Shalako. There is dancing and feasting for 24 hours. Some of the Zunis wear tall, colorful bird masks at the ceremony.

# NEW YORK

The first U.S. capital was New York City. George Washington was inaugurated there in 1789. It is said that Washington called the state "the seat of empire." New York's nickname quickly became the Empire State.

New York City is the largest city in the country. People from many different countries settled there. It is the center of many different industries, such as banking, television, and the stock market. Some of the most famous sights in the city are the Empire State Building, the Statue of Liberty, the United Nations building, and the World Trade Center. New York City's nickname is the Big Apple.

The Erie Canal helped make the state an important industrial center. The canal took eight years to build. It was finished in 1825. The Erie Canal connected the Atlantic Ocean to the Great Lakes. Part of the canal is open for tourists to see.

New York State has beautiful lakes, mountains, forests, and resorts. Besides New York City, Niagara Falls is the state's biggest tourist attraction. Two of the Great Lakes border New York—Lake Ontario and Lake Erie. There are six long thin lakes in the center of the state called the Finger Lakes. These are popular for vacations.

Four presidents were born in New York. They were Martin Van Buren, Millard Fillmore, Theodore Roosevelt, and Franklin Delano Roosevelt.

**NEW YORK (NY)**
**Capital:** Albany
**Flower:** Rose
**Bird:** Bluebird
**Tree:** Sugar maple
**Nickname:** Empire State
**Admitted to Union:** July 26, 1788—11th State
**Land Area:** 47,831 square miles (123,882 square kilometers)
**Total Area:** 49,576 square miles (128,402 square kilometers)
**1990 Population:** 17,990,455

The state of New York ranks high in manufacturing, trade with other countries, printing, publishing, clothing, and food. Its farms produce dairy products, fruits and vegetables, poultry, and grapes for wine.

## INTERESTING FACTS:
- Peter Minuit bought Manhattan Island from the Manhattan Indians in 1626. He gave them $24 worth of beads and cloth.
- Abner Doubleday of Cooperstown invented the game of baseball in 1839. The Baseball Hall of Fame is in Cooperstown.
- The U.S. Military Academy is in West Point. New officers go to college there.

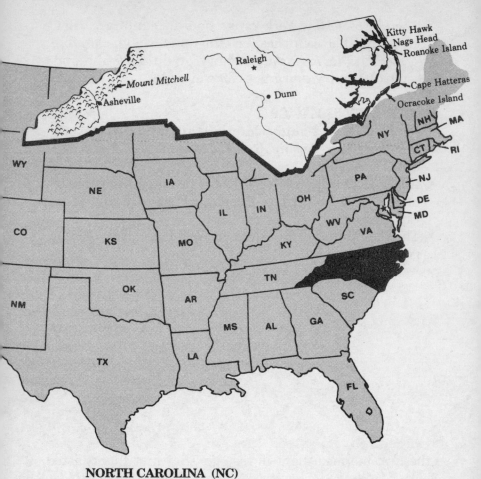

## NORTH CAROLINA (NC)

**Capital:** Raleigh
**Flower:** Flowering dogwood
**Bird:** Cardinal
**Tree:** Pine
**Nickname:** Tar Heel State
**Admitted to Union:** November 21, 1789—12th State
**Land Area:** 48,798 square miles (126,387 square kilometers)
**Total Area:** 52,586 square miles (136,197 square kilometers)
**1990 Population:** 6,628,637

# NORTH CAROLINA

Sir Walter Raleigh sent colonists to Roanoke Island in 1585 and 1587. Virginia Dare was the first English child born in America. The child's grandfather was the governor of the colony. When he returned from a trip back to England, the colony was gone. No one knows what happened to the colonists. Every summer, a play called *The Lost Colony* is performed on the island to tell this story.

A long, thin piece of land runs along North Carolina's Atlantic coastline. This is called the Outer Banks. Nags Head and Cape Hatteras have beautiful unspoiled beaches. The tallest lighthouse in the U.S. is at Cape Hatteras. It is 208 feet (63.4 meters) tall. There have been hundreds of shipwrecks off the cape.

The Wright brothers used the sand dunes at Kill Devil Hill near Kitty Hawk in 1903. Their small airplane made the first manned flight in history. That first flight lasted just 12 seconds. Today the same sand dunes are used for flying hang gliders.

North Carolina is first in the country in production of furniture, textiles, bricks, tobacco, mica, and lithium. It is a leading producer of corn, cotton, peanuts, hay, and vegetables. Tourists spend more than one billion dollars every year in North Carolina.

Mount Mitchell is the tallest mountain in the U.S. east of the Mississippi River. It is 6,684 feet (2,037 meters) high.

Grandfather Mountain is thought to be the oldest mountain in the world. The Blue Ridge Mountains are in the western part of the state.

Three U.S. presidents were born in North Carolina. Andrew Jackson, James K. Polk, and Andrew Johnson Jackson was born near the border of North and South Carolina. Both states claim his birthplace as their own.

## INTERESTING FACTS:

- Blackbeard the pirate is said to have had his headquarters on Ocracoke Island in the late 1600s and early 1700s. He was killed there in 1718. Many people believe his treasure is still buried on the island.
- The National Hollerin' Contest is held every year in the town of Dunn. It is sponsored by the Spivey's Corner Volunteer Fire Department.
- The largest house in the U.S. is the Biltmore mansion in Asheville. It has 250 rooms and was built in 1895. The house is open to the public for tours.
- In 1989 Hurricane Hugo struck the Carolinas. It killed 49 Americans and left many more homeless.

# NORTH DAKOTA

The Badlands of North Dakota are one of the most famous places in the state. Strange shapes of clay and stone were formed by erosion. Water and wind formed these hills and peaks over thousands of years.

Theodore Roosevelt lived in North Dakota for a few years as a young man. He owned two ranches there and lived in a cabin. He later chose a western name for his cavalry in the Spanish-American War. Teddy Roosevelt and his Rough Riders became famous. Theodore Roosevelt became the twenty-sixth president in 1901. There is a national park in the Badlands named for him.

The capitol building in Bismarck is a surprise. It doesn't have a dome or pillars like many capitols. It is a 19-story skyscraper. Teddy Roosevelt's ranch cabin has been moved to the grounds of the capitol.

North Dakota is the most rural of all the states. More than 90 percent of its land is farmland. North Dakota farms produce wheat, rye, flax, barley, hay, and many other crops. There are many large cattle ranches. The soil is so rich that it is joked that a nail planted in North Dakota would grow into a crowbar.

Other products of the state are processed foods, farm equipment, oil products, clay, sand, and gravel.

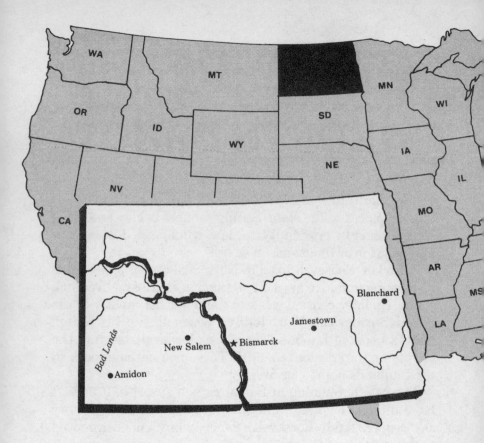

**NORTH DAKOTA (ND)**
**Capital:** Bismarck
**Flower:** Wild prairie rose
**Bird:** Western meadow lark
**Tree:** American elm
**Nicknames:** Sioux State, Flickertail State
**Admitted to Union:** November 2, 1889—39th State
**Land Area:** 69,273 square miles (179,417 square kilometers)
**Total Area:** 70,665 square miles (183,022 square kilometers)
**1990 Population:** 638,800

## INTERESTING FACTS:

- The world's largest buffalo is near Jamestown. It is a concrete statue that is 20 feet (six meters) tall. The world's largest statue of a cow is on a hill near New Salem. It is 38 feet (11.58 meters) tall.
- Near the town of Amidon are some unusual underground coal beds. They have been burning for many years.
- The tallest man-made structure in the U.S. is near Blanchard. The KTHI-TV tower is 2,063 feet (629 meters) tall.

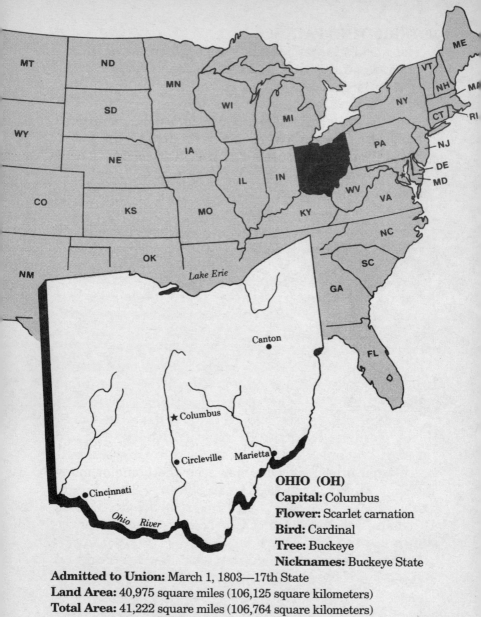

**OHIO (OH)**
**Capital:** Columbus
**Flower:** Scarlet carnation
**Bird:** Cardinal
**Tree:** Buckeye
**Nicknames:** Buckeye State

**Admitted to Union:** March 1, 1803—17th State
**Land Area:** 40,975 square miles (106,125 square kilometers)
**Total Area:** 41,222 square miles (106,764 square kilometers)
**1990 Population:** 10,847,115

# OHIO

The first permanent settlement in Ohio was Marietta. It was named for Queen Marie Antoinette of France. A group of 47 settlers started the town in 1788. Cincinnati was also started that year. At first it was called Losantiville.

Most of the early settlers came down the Ohio River on flatboats. The trip was dangerous because of pirates and Indians. Almost 70,000 people arrived in Ohio in the 15 years before it became a state. Ohio was the first state west of the Allegheny Mountains.

The first steamboat began to operate on Lake Erie in 1817. Its name was *Walk-in-the-Water*. The Erie Canal opened in 1825. This helped the growth of Ohio's industries.

Seven presidents were born in Ohio. They were Grant, Hayes, Garfield, Benjamin Harrison, McKinley, Taft, and Harding. William Henry Harrison lived in Ohio when he was elected president. Ohio has been the home of many famous inventors, such as Thomas Edison and the Wright brothers. John Glenn and Neil Armstrong are two famous astronauts from Ohio. John Glenn became a senator for the state in 1974.

Ohio is a leading manufacturing state. Major products are iron, steel, rubber products, auto parts, machinery, and glass. The state is a leader in the production of sandstone, clay, salt, and gravel. Ohio's many farms are known for dairy products, sheep, hogs, popcorn, and hothouse vegetables.

**INTERESTING FACTS:**

- The Indians thought that buckeye nuts looked like the eyes of a deer. They called the nuts buckeyes. William Henry Harrison gave away canes made of buckeye wood in his campaign for president. Ohio became known as the Buckeye State.
- The Pro Football Hall of Fame is in Canton. The College Football Hall of Fame is in Cincinnati.
- The Rock 'n' Roll Hall of Fame opened in Cleveland in June of 1993.
- Every year thousands of people visit the town of Circleville for its Pumpkin Festival. You can eat a pumpkinburger, pumpkin ice cream, or a piece of the world's largest pumpkin pie.

# OKLAHOMA

The name *Oklahoma* comes from the Choctaw Indian word for "red people." There are more Indians in Oklahoma than in any other state. There are no reservations there today. But between 1834 and 1889 the whole state was known as Indian Territory. Only Indians could live there.

The U.S. government forced most of the Indians in the southeastern states to move to Indian Territory. The roads the Indians followed to get there are known as the Trail of Tears. Many of the Indians died before reaching Oklahoma.

In 1889 the territory was opened to settlers. Thousands of people lined up on the border. When the signal was given, they raced into the territory to claim their land. Some people went in early to claim their land. They became known as Sooners.

Will Rogers was one of the state's most famous men. He was a circus performer and a radio and movie star. He wrote many funny articles for newspapers and magazines. The American people loved him. He was killed in an airplane crash in 1935.

Oklahoma is an oil state. There are producing oil wells on the grounds of the state capitol building. Tulsa is called the Oil Capital of the World. The headquarters of close to a thousand oil companies are located there. There are many pipelines under the state to carry oil and natural gas.

Manufacturing, minerals, and agriculture are also

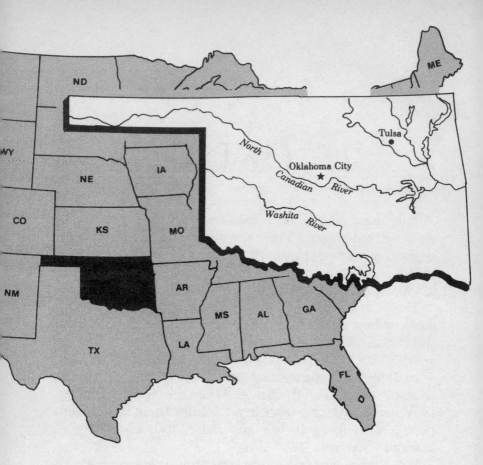

**OKLAHOMA (OK)**
**Capital:** Oklahoma City
**Flower:** Mistletoe
**Bird:** Scissor-tailed flycatcher
**Tree:** Redbud
**Nickname:** Sooner State
**Admitted to Union:** November 16, 1907—46th State
**Land Area:** 68,782 square miles (178,145 square kilometers)
**Total Area:** 69,919 square miles (181,089 square kilometers)
**1990 Population:** 3,145,585

important to Oklahoma. The major agricultural products are wheat, cattle, cotton, grains, and nuts.

**INTERESTING FACTS:**
- The state of Oklahoma is shaped something like a side view of a cooking pan. The narrow piece of land on the western side of the state is called the Panhandle.
- A Cherokee Indian named Sequoya invented the Cherokee alphabet in the 1800s. Before that there was no written Cherokee language.
- The National Cowboy Hall of Fame is in Oklahoma City. Seventeen western states helped start this museum.

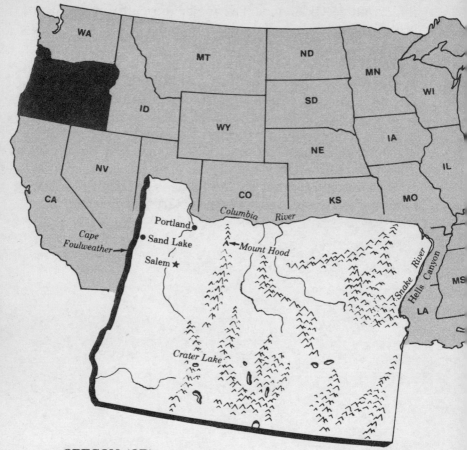

**OREGON (OR)**
**Capital:** Salem
**Flower:** Oregon grape
**Bird:** Western meadow lark
**Tree:** Douglas fir
**Nickname:** Beaver State
**Admitted to Union:** February 14, 1859—33rd State
**Land Area:** 96,184 square miles (249,117 square kilometers)
**Total Area:** 96,981 square miles (251,180 square kilometers)
**1990 Population:** 2,842,321

112

# OREGON

When Oregon became the thirty-third state, news still traveled slowly. It took a month for the news to reach Salem. A telegraph message was sent to San Francisco from Washington, D.C. A steamer ship took the news to Portland. Next a rider on horseback took the message to the new state capital, Salem.

The deepest lake in the U.S. is Crater Lake. It isn't really a crater. A volcano caved in thousands of years ago and the lake was formed. Crater Lake is 1,996 feet (599 meters) deep. It is one of the bluest lakes in the world.

Oregon has several glaciers in its mountains. Hells Canyon is one of the deepest canyons in the world. It is on the border between Idaho and Oregon. The Snake River winds through the bottom of the canyon.

Washington State and Oregon are divided by the Columbia River. Dams and power plants on the major rivers provide power for Oregon's industries. There are many beautiful smaller rivers and streams for fishing and swimming.

Oregon has led the U.S. in lumber production for over 40 years. The state also leads in salmon, peppermint, pears, plums, and grass seed. The only active nickel mine in the U.S. is in Oregon.

Portland is the state's largest city. It is called the City of Roses. Mount Hood is an extinct volcano. It can be seen on

Portland's Skyline. One legend says that Paul Bunyan piled stones on his campfire. The pile of rocks became Mount Hood.

## INTERESTING FACTS:
- In 1778 Captain James Cook sailed along the Oregon coast. He named one area Cape Foul weather.
- A terrible flood swept through the Willamette Valley in 1861. The village of Champoeg was completely washed away.
- In the village of Sand Lake is Ward's Bear Park. A man named Wibb Ward has carved more than 60 large statues of bears.

# PENNSYLVANIA

King Charles II of England gave William Penn a huge grant of land in 1681. These lands became the colony of Pennsylvania. The name means "Penn's woods." Penn's colony granted important rights to the common man.

Pennsylvania is called the Birth-State of the Nation. The Continental Congresses met in Philadelphia. The Declaration of Independence was signed there. The U.S. Constitution was written there. Philadelphia was one of the U.S. capital cities before 1800. Visitors to the city can see Independence Hall, the Liberty Bell, and the Betsy Ross house.

General George Washington and his men spent the terrible winter of 1777-78 in Valley Forge. An important Civil War battle was fought at Gettysburg in 1863. The Battle of Gettysburg lasted three days. Later that year President Lincoln spoke at the dedication of a national cemetery in Gettysburg. His Gettysburg Address is one of the most famous speeches ever written.

Industry has been very important in the state's history. The world's first oil well was near Titusville. The U.S. Steel Corporation was started in Pittsburgh by Andrew Carnegie. It is one of the largest companies in the world. Pittsburgh is called the Steel City.

Pennsylvania is a leading state in steel, coal, manufacturing, chocolate, cement, glass, and wood

**PENNSYLVANIA (PA)**
**Capital:** Harrisburg
**Flower:** Mountain laurel
**Bird:** Ruffed grouse
**Tree:** Hemlock
**Nickname:** Keystone State
**Admitted to Union:** December 12, 1787—2nd State
**Land Area:** 44,966 square miles (116,462 square kilometers)
**Total Area:** 45,333 square miles (117,412 square kilometers)
**1990 Population:** 11,881,643

116

products. The state's many farms produce mushrooms, milk, chickens, and grains.

**INTERESTING FACTS:**
- Dr. Benjamin Franklin was Philadelphia's most famous citizen in the 1700s. He invented the Franklin stove, the lightning rod, and bifocal glasses.
- The South Fork Dam near Johnstown broke in May 1889. Over 2,000 people were killed in the flood.
- Hershey has the world's largest chocolate factory. The town's main streets are Cocoa Avenue and Chocolate Avenue.

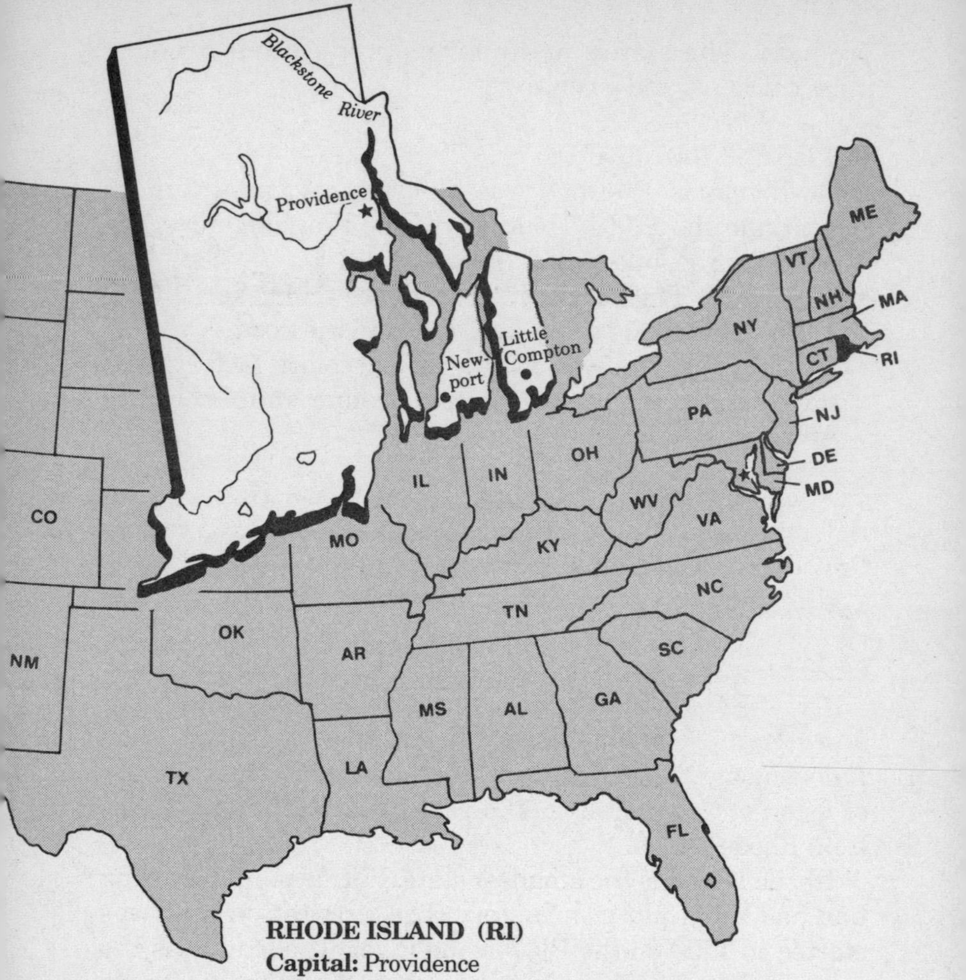

**RHODE ISLAND (RI)**

**Capital:** Providence
**Flower:** Violet
**Bird:** Rhode Island Red
**Tree:** Red maple
**Nicknames:** Ocean State, Little Rhody
**Admitted to Union:** May 29, 1790—13th State
**Land Area:** 1,049 square miles (2,717 square kilometers)
**Total Area:** 1,214 square miles (3,144 square kilometers)
**1990 Population:** 1,003,464

# RHODE ISLAND

Roger Williams started the colony of Rhode Island in 1636. He had been forced out of the Massachusetts colony because of his religious beliefs. His new colony allowed freedom of religion. Williams believed the Indians had rights to the land. The first settlement in Rhode Island was Providence Plantations.

Rhode Island signed its own Declaration of Independence in May of 1776. During the Revolutionary War, several battles took place in the state.

The state capitol building in Providence has a dome with a statue of a man on top. The statue is called "The Independent Man." Inside the capitol is the famous picture of George Washington by Gilbert Stuart. The artist was from Rhode Island.

Rhode Island is the smallest state. But its manufacturing has had a big place in history. The first cotton mill was started in 1790 on the Blackstone River. The state was the center of the textile industry in the 1800s. Today Rhode Island leads the U.S. in wool, lace, silver products, and jewelry. Agriculture and commercial fishing are other important industries.

Rhode Island has more than twice as many people as Alaska. But Alaska's size is big enough to make 500 Rhode Islands. The farms of Rhode Island produce 20 times as much produce as those in Alaska.

Newport is a famous resort town. Many huge summer houses were built there. Some of these houses look almost like castles. The America's Cup sailing race is held near Newport.

## INTERESTING FACTS:
- William Blackstone was a hermit who moved to the area that is now Rhode Island in 1635. Legends say he planted apple trees and rode a bull for transportation.
- The state's official name is the State of Rhode Island and Providence Plantations. Rhode Island has the longest official name, the smallest land area, and the shortest motto. The motto is "Hope."
- A new kind of chicken was developed at Little Compton in the 1800s. The Rhode Island Red became the state bird in 1954.

# SOUTH CAROLINA

Charles II of England made a large grant of land to eight of his friends in the 1600s. The area was named Carolina. Charles Towne was one of the first permanent settlements. Its name was later changed to Charleston.

Many pirates sailed off the Carolina coast in the early days of the colony. Blackbeard and Stede Bonnet were two of the most famous. A huge roundup of pirates took place in Charleston. Forty-nine pirates were executed in one month.

Over 100 battles of the Revolutionary War were fought in South Carolina. Men from South Carolina fought in most of these battles without help from the other colonies. Many of these battles were fought against Cherokee Indians fighting for the British.

The Civil War began in Charleston in 1861. Confederate troops from South Carolina fired on Fort Sumter. South Carolina was the first state to secede (withdraw) from the Union. The state's coast was blockaded during the Civil War by the North.

Charleston is famous for its many beautiful gardens. The city had the first American public museum, symphony orchestra, and department store. A dance named after the town was popular in the 1920s.

South Carolina used to be mainly a farming state. But today manufacturing is even more important than agriculture. Leading products are textiles, wood, sand,

**SOUTH CAROLINA (SC)**
**Capital:** Columbia
**Flower:** Carolina jessamine
**Bird:** Carolina wren
**Tree:** Palmetto
**Nickname:** Palmetto State
**Admitted to Union:** May 23, 1788—8th State
**Land Area:** 30,225 square miles (78,283 square kilometers)
**Total Area:** 31,055 square miles (80,432 square kilometers)
**1990 Population:** 3,486,703

glass, and asbestos. Major crops are tobacco, soybeans, corn, cotton, peaches, and hay.

**INTERESTING FACTS:**
- On Pawley's Island an old legend is told about a Gray Man ghost. He is supposed to warn people when storms are coming.
- In Georgetown you can visit the Rice Museum to learn how rice is grown. The first rice in the U.S. was grown near Charleston.
- General Francis Marion was a famous Revolutionary War leader. He learned how to fight in the wars with the Cherokees. His nickname was the Swamp Fox.

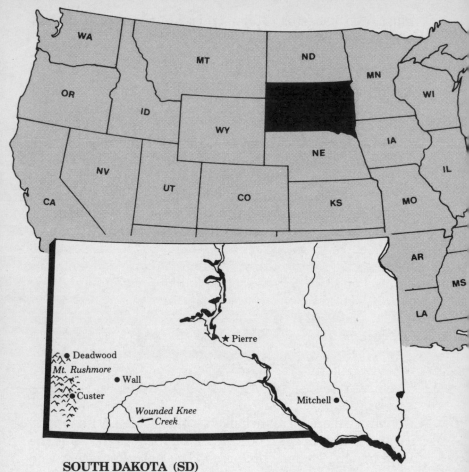

**SOUTH DAKOTA (SD)**
**Capital:** Pierre
**Flower:** American pasqueflower
**Bird:** Ring-necked pheasant
**Tree:** Black Hills spruce
**Nicknames:** Coyote State, Sunshine State
**Admitted to Union:** November 2, 1889—40th State
**Land Area:** 75,955 square miles (196,723 square kilometers)
**Total Area:** 77,047 square miles (199,551 square kilometers)
**1990 Population:** 696,004

# SOUTH DAKOTA

Gold was discovered in the Black Hills of South Dakota in 1874. A soldier with General George A. Custer found the gold near the town of Custer. Thousands of people went to the Black Hills looking for gold. Deadwood became a boom town in 1876 after gold was discovered there. Many famous outlaws and frontiersmen arrived, like Calamity Jane and Wild Bill Hickok.

The Dakota Territory got its name from an Indian word. *Dakotah* is the Sioux word for "friends working together." The Indians didn't like the settlers coming into the territory. The Indians and the Army had many battles. The last major Indian battle was fought at Wounded Knee Creek in 1890.

One of America's most famous sights is Mount Rushmore in the Black Hills. The faces of Presidents George Washington, Thomas Jefferson, Theodore Roosevelt, and Abraham Lincoln are carved in the side of the mountain. Dynamite was used to blast the granite into shape. It is the largest sculpture in the world.

An even larger sculpture is being carved near Custer. It will show Chief Crazy Horse riding on a horse. Work on the statue began in 1948 and is still not complete.

The Badlands of South Dakota are an area of strange stone shapes created by erosion. It is one of the best areas in the world for finding fossils of prehistoric animals.

South Dakota is called the Pheasant Capital of the World. There are more than ten million pheasants in the state. Agriculture is the state's most important industry. South Dakota is a leader in grains, livestock, and processed foods. The Homestake gold mine is the largest in the U.S.

**INTERESTING FACTS:**
- The largest herd of buffalo in the U.S. is at Custer State Park.
- The Wall Drug Store in the town of Wall has been advertised all over the world. There is a huge statue of a dinosaur outside the store.
- The Corn Palace is in Mitchell. It is decorated with pictures made from ears of corn. The Corn Palace Festival is held there every year.

# TENNESSEE

In 1846 the U.S. was at war with Mexico. Over 30,000 men from Tennessee volunteered for this war. Tennessee earned its nickname of the Volunteer State because of this.

The Tennessee Valley Authority (TVA) was a government project started in the 1930s. The TVA built dams on the Tennessee River in seven southern states. The dams provide irrigation, power, and flood control. The Norris Dam in Tennessee was the first TVA dam.

The 1982 World's Fair was held in Knoxville. Millions of people visited exhibits from 34 countries. The Sunsphere is a huge gold ball 226 feet (68.9 meters) high. There is a restaurant inside. The Sunsphere was built for the fair at a cost of $8.5 million.

Nashville is the home of country music. The Grand Ole Opry and the Country Music Hall of Fame are there. Nashville is the second biggest recording center in the country.

Memphis was Elvis Presley's home. His mansion, Graceland, is now open to the public. The estate costs half a million dollars a year just for upkeep.

In Chattanooga you can see the Chattanooga Choo Choo. You can ride the world's steepest passenger railroad to the top of Lookout Mountain. The Davy Crockett Birthplace is near Limestone. Gatlinburg is a resort town with lots of mountain crafts. At the Smoky Sky Lift you can ride a cable

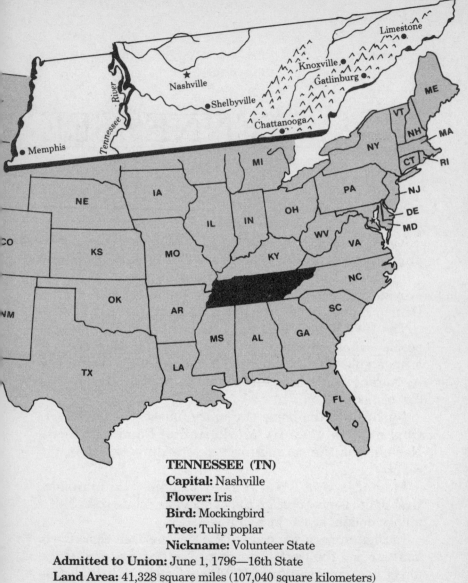

**TENNESSEE (TN)**
**Capital:** Nashville
**Flower:** Iris
**Bird:** Mockingbird
**Tree:** Tulip poplar
**Nickname:** Volunteer State
**Admitted to Union:** June 1, 1796—16th State
**Land Area:** 41,328 square miles (107,040 square kilometers)
**Total Area:** 42,244 square miles (109,412 square kilometers)
**1990 Population:** 4,877,185

car up Crockett Mountain.

Leading products of the state are tobacco, wood, chemicals, textiles, marble, and clothing. Livestock and dairy products are important in agriculture.

**INTERESTING FACTS:**
- Two presidents grew up in Tennessee. They were Andrew Johnson and James K. Polk. A third president, Andrew Jackson, lived in Tennessee when he was elected.
- The Tennessee walking horse is the official state horse. The Tennessee Walking Horse National Celebration is held every summer in Shelbyville.
- The Peabody Hotel in Memphis is famous for its ducks. Twice a day the ducks march through the lobby and swim in the fountain.

**TEXAS (TX)**
**Capital:** Austin
**Flower:** Bluebonnet
**Bird:** Mockingbird
**Tree:** Pecan
**Nickname:** Lone Star State
**Admitted to Union:** December 29, 1845—28th State
**Land Area:** 262,134 square miles (678,927 square kilometers)
**Total Area:** 269,339 square miles (692,408 square kilometers)
**1990 Population:** 16,986,510

# TEXAS

Texas was claimed by Spain and then by Mexico. The Texans and the Mexicans fought a war from 1835 to 1836. The most famous battle was at an old mission called the Alamo. About 150 Texans tried to hold the Alamo against thousands of Mexican soldiers. All the Texans were killed. Jim Bowie and Davy Crockett died there.

Sam Houston was one of the state's heroes. He was commander-in-chief of the Texan army. His army defeated Mexican General Santa Anna in the Battle of San Jacinto. The Texans' cry became famous: "Remember the Alamo!" Sam Houston was elected president of Texas in 1836.

The Independent Republic of Texas was a country from 1836 to 1845. In 1845 Texas joined the U.S. Texas has the right to divide into five states if it ever wants to.

The thirty-sixth president of the U.S. was Lyndon B. Johnson. He was from Johnson City, Texas. The town was named for his grandfather. Dwight D. Eisenhower was born in Denison. He was the thirty-fourth president.

Texas is the second largest state in area. It is third largest in population. Texas leads the nation in oil, cotton, sheep, cattle, and mineral production. Many ranches and farms produce peanuts, poultry, rice, pecans, fruits, and vegetables.

The state of Texas is not all flat ranch land. There are also mountains, forests, plantations, canyons, beaches, granite cliffs, rivers, lakes, and growing cities.

**INTERESTING FACTS:**

- In 1901 Galveston was hit by a terrible hurricane. About 6,000 people were killed.
- Oil was discovered near Beaumont in 1901. The first oil well there was called the Spindletop well.
- You can visit Mission Control Center at the Lyndon B. Johnson Space Center in Houston. Moon rocks, spacecraft, and skylabs are also part of the tour.

# UTAH

Utah was not explored by white men until 1776. Most of the pioneers in Utah were members of the Mormon religion. Their leader was Brigham Young. They arrived in Utah in 1847. The next year swarms of crickets started to eat all the crops. Sea gulls flew in from the Great Salt Lake and ate the crickets. The Mormons were grateful to the sea gulls for saving their food. The sea gull is now the state bird.

Most of the early towns in Utah were started by Mormons. Salt Lake City is the state capital. It is also the headquarters of the Mormon church. The Mormon Temple there took 40 years to build.

In 1869 the transcontinental railroad was finished at Promontory Point. The final two spikes were made of gold from California. When the railroad was finished, people could travel all the way west by train.

The Great Salt Lake is much more salty than the ocean. People will not sink in the water. Most people don't swim there because of the salt and pollution. There are 16 islands in the lake.

Utah has several mountains and canyons that are popular for skiing. The state also has large desert sand wilderness areas. The Bonneville salt flats are part of the Great Salt Lake Desert. Cars race there on hard salt left from an ancient lake that dried up.

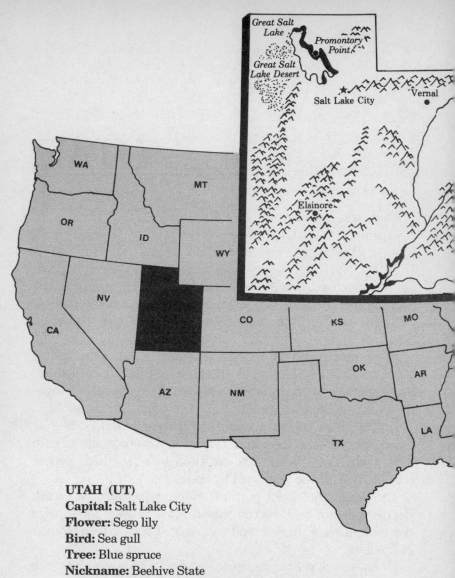

**UTAH (UT)**
**Capital:** Salt Lake City
**Flower:** Sego lily
**Bird:** Sea gull
**Tree:** Blue spruce
**Nickname:** Beehive State
**Admitted to Union:** January 4, 1896—45th State
**Land Area:** 82,096 square miles (212,629 square kilometers)
**Total Area:** 84,916 square miles (219,931 square kilometers)
**1990 Population:** 1,722,850

134

Manufacturing, mining, agriculture, and tourism are the major industries. Copper, gold, oil, sheep, and fruit are among the major products.

**INTERESTING FACTS:**
- The only place in the U.S. where four states come together in a corner point is the southeast corner of Utah. The other states are Colorado, New Mexico, and Arizona.
- At the Fieldhouse of Natural History in Vernal there is a huge model of a dinosaur. Dippy the Diplodocus is 76 feet (23 meters) long.
- The small town of Elsinore didn't have a public library. In 1980 a 12-year-old boy started one himself.

**VERMONT (VT)**
**Capital:** Montpelier
**Flower:** Red clover
**Bird:** Hermit thrush
**Tree:** Sugar maple

**Nickname:** Green Mountain State
**Admitted to Union:** March 4, 1791—14th State
**Land Area:** 9,276 square miles (24,025 square kilometers)
**Total Area:** 9,609 square miles (24,887 square kilometers)
**1990 Population:** 562,758

# VERMONT

Vermont is a state of small towns, dairy farms, maple trees, and snow-covered mountains. Burlington is the largest town. But only about 39,000 people live there.

The state's name comes from the French words for green mountain—*vert mont*. The Green Mountains and the Taconics are the state's two mountain ranges. Tourists enjoy famous ski areas like Stowe, Mount Snow, and Sugarbush.

In the 1760s New York claimed the land that is now Vermont. Ethan Allen and his Green Mountain Boys fought against these claims. During the Revolutionary War the Green Mountain Boys captured Fort Ticonderoga while the British soldiers were sleeping.

In 1777 Vermont declared itself an independent state. It was a separate republic until 1791 when it became the fourteenth state.

Two U.S. presidents were born in Vermont. Chester Arthur was the twenty-first president. Calvin Coolidge was the thirtieth president. He was the only president born on Independence Day.

Vermont leads the U.S. in maple syrup production. There are more than three million sugar maple trees in the state. Maple syrup is made by boiling many gallons of sap down to thick syrup. Other important products from Vermont are cattle, asbestos, granite, marble, and slate.

Morgan horses were the first breed developed in the U.S. All Morgans are related to a Vermont stallion named Justin Morgan. The stallion was named after his owner.

**INTERESTING FACTS:**
- In the town of Barre you can visit a Maple Museum to see how maple syrup and sugar are made.
- The oldest log cabin in the U.S. is the Hyde Log Cabin on Grand Isle. It was built in 1783.
- Rudyard Kipling and Robert Frost are two famous authors who lived in Vermont.

# VIRGINIA

Jamestown was the first permanent English settlement in North America. It was founded in 1607. Williamsburg was the capital of Virginia from 1699 to 1779. Many old buildings there have been restored and are open to the public. You can see how people lived and worked in the 1700s.

Many Civil War battles were fought in Virginia. Richmond became the capital of the Confederacy in 1861. Part of the state broke away during the war and became West Virginia. General Robert E. Lee surrendered to General Ulysses S. Grant at Appomattox.

Virginia is known as the Mother of Presidents. Eight U.S. presidents were born in Virginia. They were Washington, Jefferson, Madison, Monroe, W. H. Harrison, Tyler, Taylor, and Wilson.

The College of William and Mary is the second oldest college in the U.S. Three presidents went to school there: Jefferson, Monroe, and Tyler. The University of Virginia was founded by Thomas Jefferson. He designed some of the buildings there.

Mount Vernon was George Washington's estate. He and his wife are buried there. Thomas Jefferson's home, Monticello, is near Charlottesville. He designed the house himself and it took 41 years to finish.

Important products of Virginia are seafood, hams,

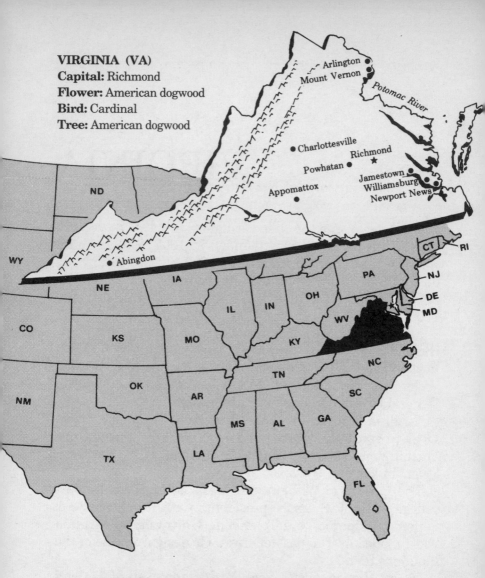

**VIRGINIA (VA)**
**Capital:** Richmond
**Flower:** American dogwood
**Bird:** Cardinal
**Tree:** American dogwood

Arlington
Mount Vernon
Potomac River

Charlottesville
Powhatan · Richmond ★
Jamestown
Appomattox · Williamsburg
Newport News

ND

WY
Abingdon
NE
IA
CT
RI
PA
NJ
IL
IN
OH
DE
MD
CO
KS
MO
WV
KY
NC
OK
TN
NM
AR
SC
MS
AL
GA
TX
LA
FL

**Nicknames:** Old Dominion, Mother of Presidents
**Admitted to Union:** June 25, 1788—10th State
**Land Area:** 39,780 square miles (103,030 square kilometers)
**Total Area:** 40,817 square miles (105,716 square kilometers)
**1990 Population:** 6,187,358

tobacco, peanuts, and turkeys. Ships and submarines are built in Newport News.

Arlington National Cemetery is just across the Potomac River from Washington, D.C. The Tomb of the Unknown Soldier is located there.

## INTERESTING FACTS:
- The world's only spider museum is in the town of Powhatan. You can see a tarantula and a collection of spider webs.
- The Pentagon Building in Arlington is the world's largest office building. Almost 30,000 people work there.
- The Barter Theater is in Abingdon. During the Depression people could bring food to barter (trade) for a ticket.

**WASHINGTON (WA)**
**Capital:** Olympia
**Flower:** Rhododendron
**Bird:** Willow goldfinch
**Tree:** Western hemlock
**Nickname:** Evergreen State
**Admitted to Union:** November 11, 1889—42nd State
**Land Area:** 66,570 square miles (172,416 square kilometers)
**Total Area:** 68,192 square miles (176,616 square kilometers)
**1990 Population:** 4,866,692

# WASHINGTON

The Oregon Territory was formed by Congress in 1848. It included Oregon, Washington, and part of Idaho. Early settlers followed the Oregon Trail in their covered wagons. So many people arrived that a separate Washington Territory was created in 1853. In 1889, Washington became the only state named for a president.

Washington is rich in natural resources. It has a greater waterpower capacity than any other state. The Grand Coulee Dam is the largest concrete dam in the U.S. Fishing and lumber products are major industries.

There are three mountain ranges in the state: the Blue Mountains, the Cascade Mountains, and the Olympic Mountains. Mount Rainier is the highest mountain in Washington. In March 1980, Mount St. Helens became an active volcano. In May the volcano erupted and 61 people were killed.

Seattle is the largest city in the state. The 1962 World's Fair was held there. The Space Needle was built for the fair. It is a 600-foot (183-meter) tower with an outside elevator. The revolving restaurant on top is called the Eye of the Needle.

Washington is a leading producer of apples, pears, lumber, aluminum, fish, and flower bulbs. The Boeing Company builds 747 and 727 jets. There are several large shipyards. The Puget Sound Naval Shipyard is the largest shipyard on the Pacific Coast.

**INTERESTING FACTS:**
- The tallest totem pole in the world is in Tacoma. It was carved by Alaskan Indians.
- Ice Cave is a "bubble cave" near Mount Adams. It was formed when a big air bubble puffed up molten lava.
- The World Indoor Paper Airplane Championships are held every year in Seattle. In 1982 there were over 5,300 contestants.

# WEST VIRGINIA

West Virginia has the highest altitude of any state east of the Mississippi River. Almost the whole state is covered with mountains or hills. West Virginia is part of the region called Appalachia. Its mountains are the Appalachian and the Allegheny Mountains. Over three-quarters of the state is forest.

Coal mining is the state's largest industry. There are billions of tons of coal still waiting to be mined. West Virginia is also a leader in tobacco, lumber, chemicals, glass, and steel. The state has a moderate climate, so many kinds of crops grow well there. Golden Delicious apples were developed from a West Virginia tree.

Charleston and Huntington are the largest cities. Huntington is a busy port city on the Ohio River. West Virginia's rivers give the state a huge supply of fresh water. White-water rafting is popular on the New and Gauley Rivers. There are several mineral springs in West Virginia. Some people think the waters help in healing.

In 1859, John Brown and his men captured the U.S. arsenal at Harpers Ferry. Brown was protesting slavery. He was executed for treason.

During the Civil War, the western counties of Virginia broke away to form a new state. West Virginia joined the Union in 1863. Several Civil War battles were fought in West Virginia.

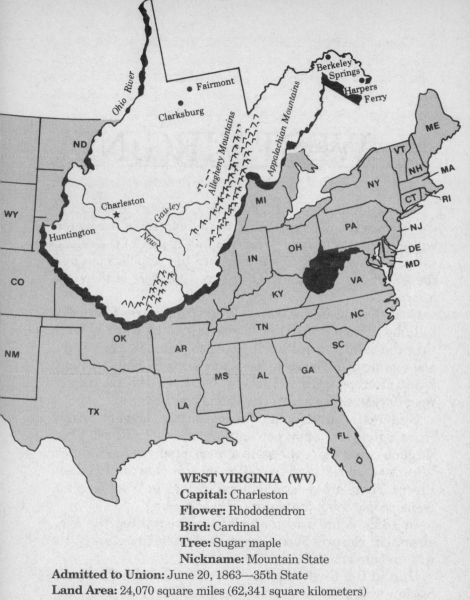

**WEST VIRGINIA (WV)**
**Capital:** Charleston
**Flower:** Rhododendron
**Bird:** Cardinal
**Tree:** Sugar maple
**Nickname:** Mountain State
**Admitted to Union:** June 20, 1863—35th State
**Land Area:** 24,070 square miles (62,341 square kilometers)
**Total Area:** 24,181 square miles (62,628 square kilometers)
**1990 Population:** 1,793,477

One of the Confederacy's famous generals was Stonewall Jackson. He was born in Clarksburg, West Virginia. Jackson got his nickname of Stonewall at the first Battle of Bull Run. His defense was "like a stone wall." Jackson's leadership was very important to the South.

**INTERESTING FACTS:**
- Two West Virginia women were spies for the Confederacy during the Civil War. They were Belle Boyd and Nancy Hart.
- The town of Fairmont has a bug factory. Models of insects are made in all shapes and sizes.
- The oldest castle in the U.S. is Berkeley Castle near the town of Berkeley Springs. It was built in 1885. It was built to look like Berkeley Castle in England.

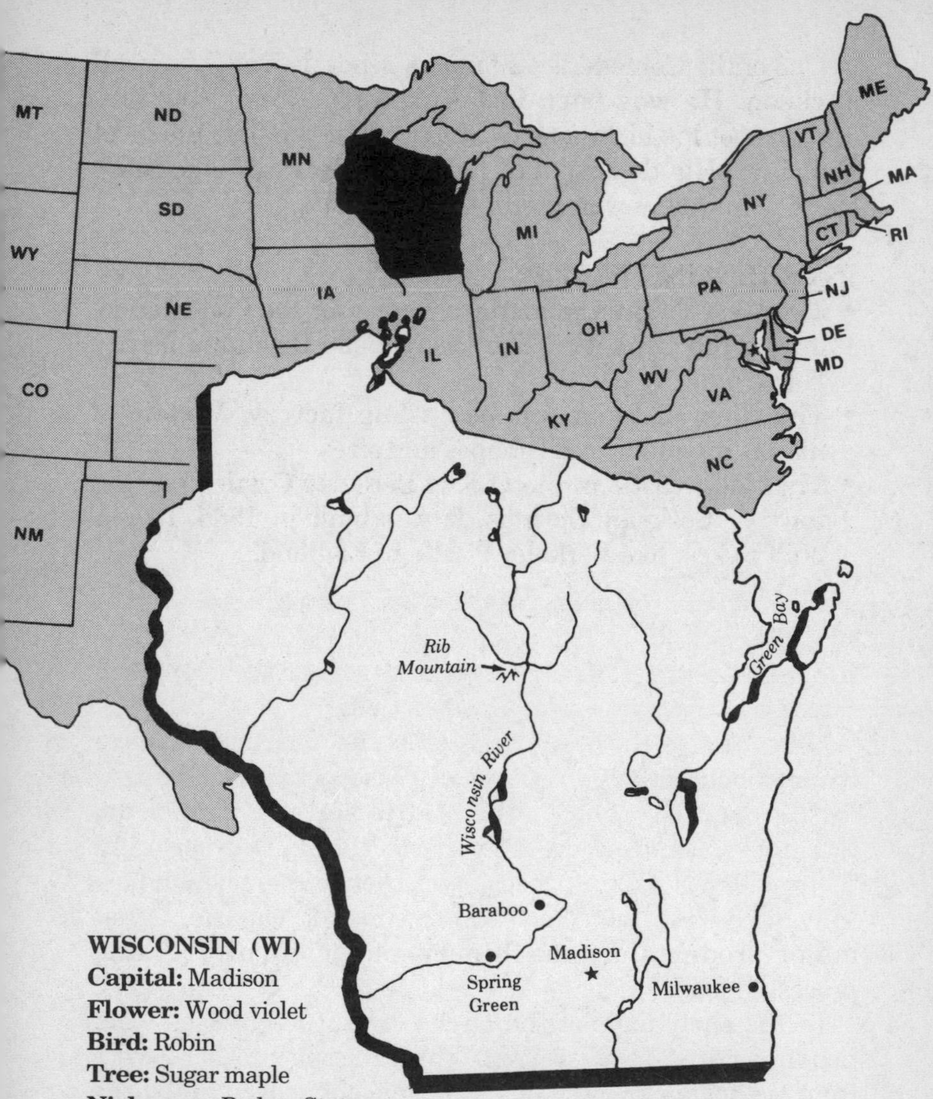

**WISCONSIN (WI)**
**Capital:** Madison
**Flower:** Wood violet
**Bird:** Robin
**Tree:** Sugar maple
**Nickname:** Badger State
**Admitted to Union:** May 29, 1848—30th State
**Land Area:** 54,464 square miles (141,062 square kilometers)
**Total Area:** 56,154 square miles (145,438 square kilometers)
**1990 Population:** 4,891,769

# WISCONSIN

Wisconsin's name comes from the Indian words for "where the waters gather." There are over 10,000 streams and 8,000 lakes in the state. One story says the giant lumberman, Paul Bunyan, jumped from Rib Mountain into the Wisconsin River. The splash was so big it made lakes all over the state.

With all those lakes, Wisconsin is a popular vacation spot. Tourists enjoy waterskiing, sailing, and fishing in the summer. In the winter cross-country skiing, down-hill skiing, and ice-boating are all popular.

Wisconsin is the leading dairy state. There are almost two million milk cows in the state. Wisconsin is also famous for its cheese. Many of the state's settlers were from Germany, Scandinavia, and Switzerland. They brought their skills for making cheese and beer to their new home. Milwaukee is called the Nation's Brewing Capital. Other major products are machinery, paper, furniture, and processed foods.

In the early days of the circus, over 100 circuses were headquartered in Wisconsin. The Ringling brothers were from the town of Baraboo. Their huge circus was called the Greatest Show on Earth. There is a Circus World Museum in Baraboo.

One of the world's most famous architects was from Spring Green, Wisconsin. Frank Lloyd Wright designed some very unusual buildings. Some people dislike his work. Others think he was a genius.

The state's capital is Madison. It was named for President James Madison. The state capitol building has an unusual design. Four wings of equal size form the main building.

## INTERESTING FACTS:

- An unusual Indian mound is near Baraboo. It is shaped like a man 150 feet (about 45 meters) tall.
- Three Wisconsin men, C. Latham Sholes, Carlos Glidden, and S. W. Soulé, designed the first practical typewriter in 1867. They spent six years working on their idea.
- The first race between two automobiles took place in 1869. Two "horseless carriages" raced between Green Bay and Madison. The winner's average speed was six miles (about 9.6 kilometers) per hour.

# WYOMING

There were 12 different Indian groups living in Wyoming when the first Europeans arrived. The first settlers were fur traders. Many Mormons crossed Wyoming on their way to Utah. Many others traveled through on their way to California to look for gold. By the 1880s large cattle and horse ranches had been started in Wyoming. Towns like Laramie and Cheyenne were part of the rough life of the Wild West.

Buffalo Bill Cody founded the town of Cody in 1897. There is a large statue of him there, astride his favorite horse, Smoky. You can visit the Buffalo Bill Museum.

Wyoming is called the Equality State and its motto is "Equal Rights." The state was the first to give women the right to vote. Wyoming had the first woman justice of the peace. Texas and Wyoming elected the first women governors on the same day. One of the most famous frontier scouts was a woman named Martha Jane Canary. Her nickname was Calamity Jane.

In 1872 Congress made Yellowstone the first national park. There are about 3,000 hot springs and geysers in the park. The most famous geyser is Old Faithful. It shoots water into the air every 65 minutes. The largest Yellowstone geyser is Giant Geyser. There are also thousands of acres preserved for wildlife.

More beautiful scenery is nearby at the Grand Teton

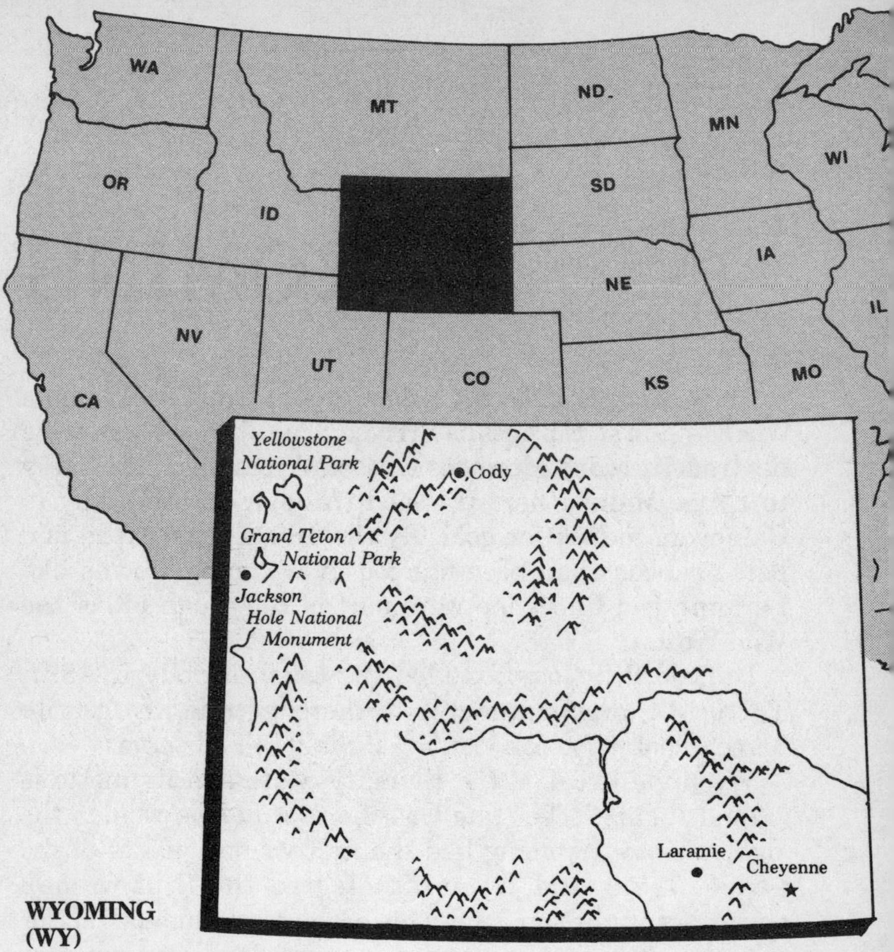
WA
OR
CA
NV
ID
MT
UT
CO
ND.
SD
NE
KS
MN
IA
WI
IL
MO
Yellowstone National Park
Cody
Grand Teton National Park
Jackson Hole National Monument
Laramie
Cheyenne

**WYOMING (WY)**

**Capital:** Cheyenne
**Flower:** Indian paintbrush
**Bird:** Meadow lark
**Tree:** Cottonwood
**Nickname:** Equality State
**Admitted to Union:** July 10, 1890—44th State
**Land Area:** 97,203 square miles (251,756 square kilometers)
**Total Area:** 97,914 square miles (253,596 square kilometers)
**1990 Population:** 453,588

National Park and Jackson Hole National Monument. The world's largest herd of elk is preserved at Jackson Hole.

Wyoming is a leader in sheep, cattle, oil, uranium, and natural gas. It is second in the U.S. in wool.

## INTERESTING FACTS:
- Buffalo Bill made the longest ride of the Pony Express when he was 15 years old. He found that his replacement had been killed. So he rode 322 miles (518.2 kilometers) across Wyoming.
- Hail falls more often in Cheyenne than in any other town in the U.S.
- The state stone is jade. The state symbol is a rider on a bucking horse.

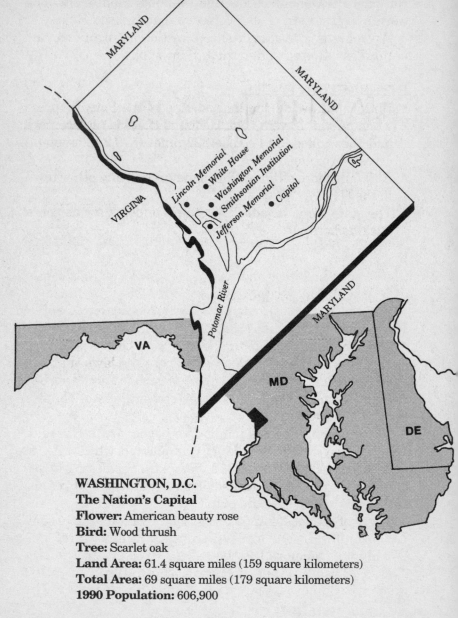

**WASHINGTON, D.C.**
**The Nation's Capital**
**Flower:** American beauty rose
**Bird:** Wood thrush
**Tree:** Scarlet oak
**Land Area:** 61.4 square miles (159 square kilometers)
**Total Area:** 69 square miles (179 square kilometers)
**1990 Population:** 606,900

# WASHINGTON, D.C.

The official name of the United States capital is Washington, the District of Columbia. The U.S. government met in eight different cities between the Revolutionary War and 1790. President Washington helped select the site for the new capital. It was a swampy area in Maryland and Virginia.

A French architect and engineer named Pierre L'Enfant designed the new capital city. It was the first national capital to be a planned city. L'Enfant put the Capitol Building on the highest hill in the center. The main streets are laid out from the Capitol like the spokes of a wheel.

Congress meets in the Capitol to pass the laws that run our government. The Capitol has a huge dome and over 500 rooms. Statuary Hall has one or two statues of famous people from each state.

The president and his family live in the White House at 1600 Pennsylvania Avenue. It was painted white after it was burned in the War of 1812. Before the repainting it was called the President's House. There are over 130 rooms. Only a few are open to the public.

Three of the most famous Washington landmarks are the Lincoln, Jefferson, and Washington Memorials. The Washington Memorial is the tallest structure in the city. The Smithsonian Institution is the nation's greatest museum. Some people call it "Uncle Sam's attic." The

National Air and Space Museum is part of the Smithsonian. You can see the Wright brothers' plane, the Apollo II command module, and moon rocks. Every spring there is a Cherry Blossom Festival in the District of Columbia. Three thousand cherry trees were planted in 1912. They were a gift from the city of Tokyo.

**INTERESTING FACTS:**
- The Bureau of Engraving and Printing prints about $40 million a day. You can tour the building and buy $150 of shredded old money for 50 cents.
- The only panda in the U.S. is at the National Zoo. Hsing-Hsing was one of two pandas presented as a gift from China. Unfortunately Ling-Ling, the other panda, died in 1992.
- You can see the originals of the Declaration of Independence, the U.S. Constitution, and the Bill of Rights at the National Archives.

# PUZZLES

# The World of Water

1. How many Great Lakes are there? *Five*

2. Can you name them? (Hint: HOMES contains the first letter of each lake's name) *Supirior, Huron,*
   *Michigan, Erie, Ontario*

3. Niagara Falls is between which two Great Lakes?
   *Erie* and *Ontario*

4. What is the longest river in the U.S.?
   *Mississipi River*

5. Which lake in Utah is more salty than the ocean?
   *Great Salt Lake*

6. Which ocean borders the eastern coast of the U.S.?
   *Atlantic Ocean*

7. Which ocean borders the western coast of the U.S.?
   *Pacific Ocean*

8. What body of water borders Texas, Louisiana, Mississippi, Alabama, and Florida?
   *The Gulf of Mexico*

# Capital City Word Search

Can you find and circle these capitals? The names may be horizontal, vertical, or diagonal. Some names are spelled backwards. Check off each capital on the list when you find it in the puzzle.

```
C O L U M B U S P I E R R E E
Q O Z B K C R A M S I B L F Y
L H N O T N E R T C D V A X H
I G K C B D F J H L E T N A D
N I N P O R T M V X N Z S I E
C E A C X R O G E A V H I P S
O L K U E N D N S F E H N M I
L A Z V D T O L R M R L G Y O
N R O T O S Y A A J G E A L B
I D C P K N N D O U V N X O M
Q S E C A K I S A W S A S H A
T K A B F S T E B A D T F K R
A J L O O M N I L V O W I X C
M A R N Z U Y E B N H L A N I
O T L E J S M A U G U S T A E
```

| | | |
|---|---|---|
| Albany | Dover | Pierre |
| Augusta | Frankfort | Raleigh |
| Austin | Helena | Richmond |
| Bismarck | Jackson | Salem |
| Boise | Juneau | Santa Fe |
| Boston | Lansing | Topeka |
| Columbus | Lincoln | Trenton |
| Concord | Madison | |
| Denver | Olympia | |

# State Nicknames

Can you name these states from their nicknames?

| NICKNAME | STATE |
|---|---|
| 1. Centennial State | *Colorado* |
| 2. Hoosier State | *Indiana* |
| 3. Granite State | *New Hampshire* |
| 4. Buckeye State | *Ohio* |
| 5. Sooner State | *Oklahoma* |
| 6. Land of Lincoln | *Illinois* |
| 7. Pine Tree State | *Maine* |
| 8. Land of Enchantment | *New Mexico* |
| 9. Tar Heel State | *N. Carolina* |
| 10. Land of the Midnight Sun | *Alaska* |
| 11. Sunshine State | *Florida* |
| 12. Nutmeg State | *Conneticutt* |
| 13. Show Me State | *Missouri* |
| 14. Green Mountain State | *Vermont* |
| 15. Lone Star State | *Texas* |

# Scrambled States

Can you unscramble these state names?

1. chanigmi     _michigan_

2. lorniafaci     _california_

3. mussachattess     _massachusetts_

4. riagoge     _georgia_

5. nillisoi     _illinois_

6. oohi     _ohio_

7. wen coxime     _new mexico_

8. nisnocwis     _wisconsin_

9. dohre sandli     _rhode island_

10. idanain     _indiana_

11. amokalho     _oklahoma_

12. dorialf     _florida_

# Shape of the States

Can you guess the names of these states?

1.

   *Florida*

2. *Michigan*

3. *Texas*

4. *Massachusetts*

# Trivia Brain Busters

Can you guess the names of these states from the clues given?

1. The only state named for a president is

_Washington_

2 A state's name that is also a girl's name is

_Virginia_

3. The state that is made up of two peninsulas is

_Michigan_

4. The smallest state is

_Rhode Island_

5. The state that is made up of over 100 islands is

_Hawaii_

6. Disney World is located in the state of

_Florida_

7. The 1982 World's Fair was held in the state of

_Tenesse_

8. The Declaration of Independence was signed in the state of _Pennsylvania_

9. The Civil War was started in the state of

_South Carolina_

10. President Jimmy Carter's home state is

_Georgia_

# 50 States Word Search

How many states can you find and circle? The names may be horizontal, vertical, or diagonal. Some names are even spelled backwards. (Hint: Check off each state on the list below when you find it in the puzzle.)

✓ = found twice

Alabama
Alaska
Arizona
Arkansas
California
Colorado
Connecticut
Delaware
Florida
Georgia ✓
Hawaii
Idaho
Illinois
Indiana
Iowa
Kansas
Kentucky
Louisiana
Maine
Maryland
Massachusetts
Michigan
Minnesota
Mississippi
Missouri

Montana
Nebraska
Nevada
New Hampshire
New Jersey
New Mexico
New York
North Carolina
North Dakota
Ohio
Oklahoma
Oregon
Pennsylvania
Rhode Island
South Carolina
South Dakota
Tennessee
Texas
Utah
Vermont
Virginia
Washington
West Virginia
Wisconsin
Wyoming

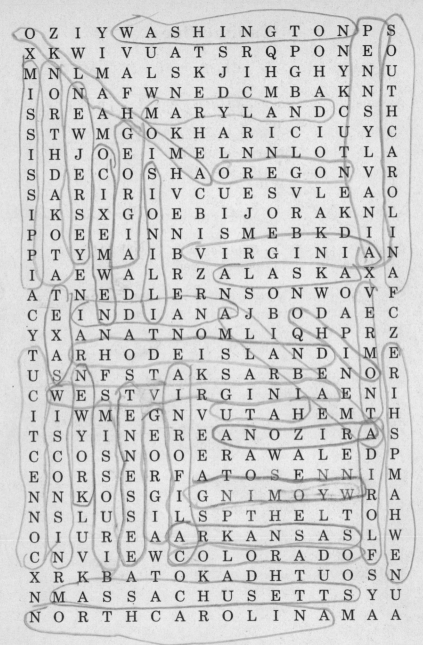

```
O Z I Y W A S H I N G T O N P S
X K W I V U A T S R Q P O N E O
M N L M A L S K J I H G H Y N U
I N N A F W N E D C M B A K N T
S R E A H M A R Y L A N D C S H
S T W M G O K H A R I C I U Y C
I H J O E I M E L N N L O T L A
S D E C S H A O R E G O N V R
S A R I R I V C U E S V L E A O
I K S X G O E B I J O R A K N L
P O E E I N N I S M E B K D I I
P T Y M A I B V I R G I N I A N
I A E W A L R Z A L A S K A X A
A T N E D L E R N S O N W O V F
C E I N D I A N A J B O D A E C
Y X A N A T N O M L I Q H P R Z
T A R H O D E I S L A N D I M E
U S N F S T A K S A R B E N O R
C W E S T V I R G I N I A E N I
I I W M E G N V U T A H E M T H
T S Y I N E R E A N O Z I R A S
C C O S N O O E R A W A L E D P
E O R S E R F A T O S E N N I M
N N K O S G I G N I M O Y W R A
N S L U S I L S P T H E L T O H
O I U R E A A R K A N S A S L W
C N V I E W C O L O R A D O F E
X R K B A T O K A D H T U O S N
N M A S S A C H U S E T T S Y U
N O R T H C A R O L I N A M A A
```

# Capital Clues

| STATE | CLUE | CAPITAL |
|-------|------|---------|
| Arkansas | a small stone | 1. _Little Rock_ |
| Nebraska | named after the president in office during the Civil War | 2. _Lincoln_ |
| Arizona | a mythical bird | 3. _Phonix_ |
| Ohio | the name of a famous explorer | 4. _Columbus_ |
| South Dakota | a French boy's name | 5. _Pierre_ |
| Utah | named for a lake | 6. _Salt Lake City_ |
| West Virginia | and old-fashioned dance | 7. _Charelston_ |
| Wisconsin | named after the fourth president | 8. _Madison_ |
| Illinois | the season after winter and a place where corn or wheat is planted | 9. _Springfield_ |
| Massachusetts | a famous tea party took place here | 10. _Boston_ |

# Scrambled States

Can you unscramble these state names?

1. ewn pahmirshe — _new hampshire_

2. sanailoui — _louisiana_

3. pannylensiav — _Pennsylvania_

4. rodacool — _Colorado_

5. wen kory — _new york_

6. goonre — _oregon_

7. viniairg — _virginia_

8. naime — _maine_

9. torhn lanaciro — _north carolina_

10. lamabaa — _alabama_

11. saxet — _texas_

12. kasala — _alaska_

13. tonmerv — _Vermont_

# Big City Match-Up

Match these large cities with the states in which they are located.

1. Atlanta *d*          a. California

2. San Francisco *a*    b. Maryland

3. Chicago *g*          c. Massachusetts

4. Detroit *j*          d. Georgia

5. Dallas *i*           e. Louisiana

6. Boston *c*           f. Ohio

7. Cleveland *f*        g. Illinois

8. Baltimore *b*        h. Colorado

9. Denver *h*           i. Texas

10. New Orleans *e*     j. Michigan

# Landmark Matching Game

Match these famous landmarks or places with the states in which they can be found.

1. Kennedy Space Center __c__          a. Arizona

2. Mount Rushmore __f__                b. Washington

3. Yosemite National Park __i__        c. Florida

4. Yellowstone National Park __j__     d. Michigan

5. Mammoth Cave __h__                  e. New York

6. Grand Canyon __a__                  f. South Dakota

7. Pearl Harbor __g__                  g. Hawaii

8. Statue of Liberty __e__             h. Kentucky

9. Mount St. Helens __b__              i. California

10. Mackinac Bridge __d__              j. Wyoming

# The Shape of the States

Can you guess the names of these states?

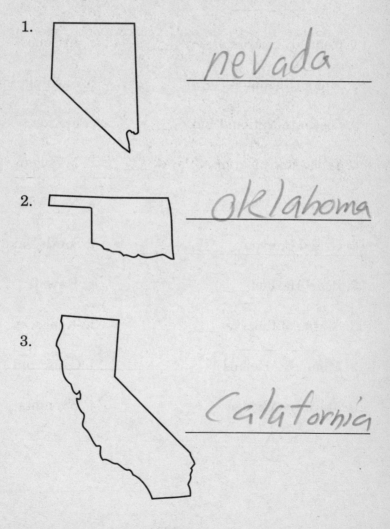

1. *nevada*

2. *oklahoma*

3. *Calafornia*

4.

tennesee

5.

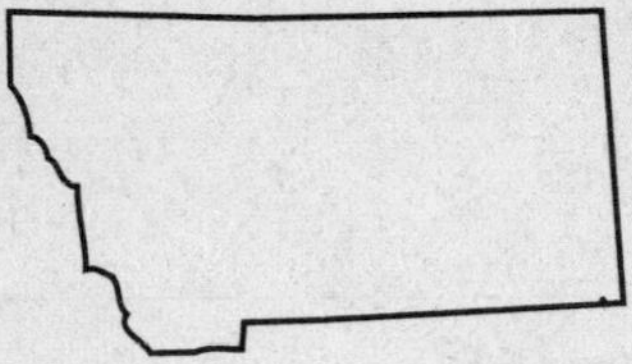

montana

6.

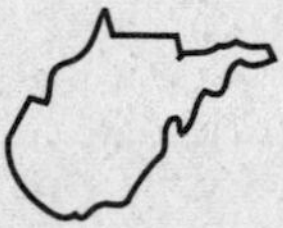

west virginia

7.

idaho

8.

maine

# ANSWERS

## The World of Water, page 158:
1. five
2. Lake Huron, Lake Ontario, Lake Michigan, Lake Erie, and Lake Superior
3. Lake Erie and Lake Ontario
4. the Mississippi
5. the Great Salt Lake
6. the Atlantic Ocean
7. the Pacific Ocean
8. the Gulf of Mexico

## Capital City Word Search, page 159:

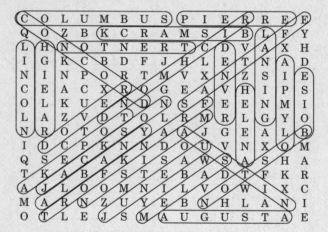

## State Nicknames, page 160:
1. Colorado, 2. Indiana, 3. New Hampshire, 4. Ohio, 5. Oklahoma, 6. Illinois, 7. Maine, 8. New Mexico, 9. North Carolina, 10. Alaska, 11. Florida, 12. Connecticut, 13. Missouri, 14. Vermont, 15. Texas

## Scrambled States, page 161:
1. Michigan, 2. California, 3. Massachusetts, 4. Georgia, 5. Illinois, 6. Ohio, 7. New Mexico, 8. Wisconsin, 9. Rhode Island, 10. Indiana, 11. Oklahoma, 12. Florida

## The Shape of the States, page 162:
1. Florida, 2. Michigan, 3. Texas, 4. Massachusetts

## Trivia Brain Busters, page 163:

1. Washington, 2. Virginia or Georgia, 3. Michigan, 4. Rhode Island,
5. Hawaii, 6. Florida, 7. Tennessee, 8. Pennyslvania, 9. South
Carolina, 10. Georgia.

## 50 States Word Search, page 164-165:

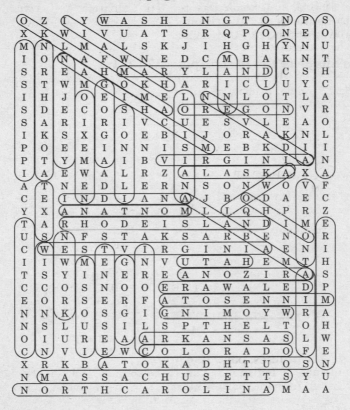

## Capital Clues, page 166:

1. Little Rock, 2. Lincoln, 3. Phoenix, 4. Columbus, 5. Pierre, 6. Salt
Lake City, 7. Charleston, 8. Madison, 9. Springfield, 10. Boston.

## Scrambled States, page 167:

1. New Hampshire, 2. Louisiana, 3. Pennsylvania, 4. Colorado,
5. New York, 6. Oregon, 7. Virginia, 8. Maine, 9. North Carolina,
10. Alabama, 11. Texas, 12. Alaska, 13. Vermont.

## Big City Match-Up, page 168:

1. (d) Georgia, 2. (a) California, 3. (g) Illinois, 4. (j) Michigan,
5. (i) Texas, 6. (c) Massachusetts, 7. (f) Ohio, 8. (b) Maryland,
9. (h) Colorado, 10. (e) Louisiana.

## Landmark Matching Game, page 169:

1. (c) Florida, 2. (f) South Dakota, 3. (i) California, 4. (j) Wyoming,
5. (h) Kentucky, 6. (a) Arizona, 7. (g) Hawaii, 8. (e) New York,
9. (b) Washington, 10. (d) Michigan.

## The Shape of the States, page 170-171:

1. Nevada, 2. Oklahoma, 3. California, 4. Tennessee, 5. Montana,
6. West Virginia, 7. Idaho, 8. Maine.